1st Workshop on Computational Neurolinguistics 2010

Held at NAACL HLT 2010

Los Angeles, California, USA
6 June 2010

ISBN: 978-1-61738-675-6

Printed from e-media with permission by:

Curran Associates, Inc.
57 Morehouse Lane
Red Hook, NY 12571

Some format issues inherent in the e-media version may also appear in this print version.

Printed by Curran Associates, Inc. (2010)

For permission requests, please contact the Association for Computational Linguistics at the address below.

Association for Computational Linguistics
209 N. Eighth Street
Stroudsburg, Pennsylvania 18360

Phone: 1-570-476-8006
Fax: 1-570-476-0860

acl@aclweb.org

Additional copies of this publication are available from:

Curran Associates, Inc.
57 Morehouse Lane
Red Hook, NY 12571 USA
Phone: 845-758-0400
Fax: 845-758-2634
Email: curran@proceedings.com
Web: www.proceedings.com

Introduction

Welcome to the NAACL-HLT 2010 Workshop on Computational Neurolinguistics.

This is the first workshop to be held on this emerging topic, which integrates recent advances in computational linguistics and cognitive neuroscience with the latest methods from machine learning. This new field promises to aid in the further development of cognitively plausible theories of language, to provide a third empirical basis as a benchmark for computational linguistics (besides corpora, and data elicited from informants), and to enrich the models of language used in neuroscience with the precision and breadth that computational linguistic methods provide. More ambitious blue-sky applications being pursued include language-based brain-computer interfaces, parsing of sentential structure from recordings of neural activity during language processing, and the derivation of language resources from neuroimaging data.

We hope that this event will provide an interdisciplinary forum for the free exchange of ideas between the participants, whose expertise ranges across computational linguistics, cognitive psychology, brain decoding, psycholinguistics and other areas of cognitive science. In preparation for the workshop we released two neural recording data-sets and corresponding language models (the CMU fMRI set and the Trento EEG set, both on a lexical semantic processing task) to allow researchers from different specialties to contribute. The papers that will be presented at the workshop cover a range of neuroimaging techniques (EEG, fMRI, MEG), models of language phenomena (distributional models of lexical semantics, formal ontologies, word class distinctions, connectionist approaches), and of machine learning and data mining methods (Bayesian learning, source separation models, regression techniques, non-linear classifiers).

In addition to the submitted papers we will have two additional talks. We are very happy to welcome Tom Mitchell to open the event. Over recent years Prof. Mitchell has chosen neuroimaging data, and language, as the two phenomena that he will focus on in his machine learning research. In addition we will give a mini-tutorial: a crash course for computational linguists in the neuroscience of language, and on basic principles of neuroimaging techniques.

Brian Murphy, Kai-min Chang, and Anna Korhonen.

Organizers:

Brian Murphy, Centre for Mind/Brain Studies, University of Trento, Italy
Kai-min Kevin Chang, Language Technologies Institute, Carnegie Mellon University, USA
Anna Korhonen, Computer Laboratory, University of Cambridge, UK

Program Committee:

Afra Alishahi, Saarland University, Germany
Ben Amsel, University of Toronto, Canada
Stefano Anzellotti, Harvard University, USA
Colin Bannard, University of Texas Austin, USA
Marco Baroni, University of Trento, Italy
Gemma Boleda, Universitat Politècnica de Catalunya, Spain
Ina Bornkessel, Max Planck Leipzig, Germany
Augusto Buchweitz, Carnegie Mellon University, USA
George Cree, University of Toronto, Canada
Barry Devereux, University of Cambridge, UK
Katrin Erk, University of Texas Austin, USA
Stefan Evert, Unversity of Osnabrück, Germany
Adele Goldberg, Princeton University, USA
Chu-Ren Huang, Hong Kong Polytechnic University, Hong Kong
Aravind Joshi, University of Pennsylvania, USA
Marcel Just, Carnegie Mellon University, USA
Frank Keller, University of Edinburgh, UK
Charles Kemp, Carnegie Mellon University, USA
Mirella Lapata, University of Edinburgh, UK
Chia-Ying Lee, Academia Sinica, Taiwan
Roger Levy, University of California Sand Diego, USA
Angelika Lingnau, University of Trento, Italy
Brad Mahon, University of Rochester, USA
Robert Mason, Carnegie Mellon University, USA
Diana McCarthy, Lexical Computing Ltd, UK
Ken McRae, University of Western Ontario, Canada
Tom Mitchell, Carnegie Mellon University, USA
Fermin Moscoso del Prado Martin, University of Provence, France
Sebastian Pado, University of Stuttgart, Germany
Francisco Pereira, Princeton University, USA
Massimo Poesio, University of Trento, Italy
Thierry Poibeau, CNRS and Ecole Normale Supérieure, France
Dean Pomerleau, Intel Labs Pittsburgh, USA
Ari Rappoport, Hebrew University of Jerusalem, Israel
Brian Roark, Oregeon Health & Science University, USA

Kenji Sagae, University of Southern California, USA
Hinrich Schuetze, Stuttgart University, Germany
Sabine Schulte im Walde, University of Stuttgart, Germany
Svetlana Shinkareva, University of South Carolina, USA
Nathaniel Smith, University of San Diego, USA
Aline Villavicencio, Federal University of Rio Grande do Sul, Brazil
David Vinson, University College London, UK
Yang ChinLung, City University of Hong Kong, China

Invited Speaker:

Tom Mitchell, Carnegie Mellon University, USA

Table of Contents

Workshop Program

Sunday, June 6, 2010

9:00–10:30 **Session I**

Invited Talk: Tom Mitchell

Learning semantic features for fMRI data from definitional text
Francisco Pereira, Matthew Botvinick and Greg Detre

10:30–11:00 **Coffee Break**

11:00–12:30 **Session II**

Concept Classification with Bayesian Multi-task Learning
Marcel van Gerven and Irina Simanova

WordNet Based Features for Predicting Brain Activity associated with meanings of nouns
Ahmad Babaeian Jelodar, Mehrdad Alizadeh and Shahram Khadivi

Network Analysis of Korean Word Associations
Jaeyoung Jung, Na Li and Hiroyuki Akama

12:30–1:30 **Lunch**

1:30–3:00 **Session III**

Detecting Semantic Category in Simultaneous EEG/MEG Recordings
Brian Murphy and Massimo Poesio

Hemispheric processing of Chinese polysemy in the disyllabic verb/ noun compounds: an event-related potential study
Chih-Ying Huang and Chia-Ying Lee

An Investigation on Polysemy and Lexical Organization of Verbs
Daniel Germann, Aline Villavicencio and Maity Siqueira

Tutorial (Part 1)

Sunday, June 6, 2010 (continued)

3:00–3:30 **Coffee Break**

3:30–5:00 **Session IV**

Tutorial (Part 2)

Acquiring Human-like Feature-Based Conceptual Representations from Corpora
Colin Kelly, Barry Devereux and Anna Korhonen

Using fMRI activation to conceptual stimuli to evaluate methods for extracting conceptual representations from corpora
Barry Devereux, Colin Kelly and Anna Korhonen

5:00–6:00 **Discussion**

Learning semantic features for fMRI data from definitional text

Francisco Pereira, Matthew Botvinick and Greg Detre
Psychology Department and Princeton Neuroscience Institute
Princeton University
Princeton, NJ 08540
{fpereira,matthewb,gdetre}@princeton.edu

Abstract

(Mitchell et al., 2008) showed that it was possible to use a text corpus to learn the value of hypothesized semantic features characterizing the meaning of a concrete noun. The authors also demonstrated that those features could be used to decompose the spatial pattern of fMRI-measured brain activation in response to a stimulus containing that noun and a picture of it. In this paper we introduce a method for learning such semantic features automatically from a text corpus, without needing to hypothesize them or provide any proxies for their presence on the text. We show that those features are effective in a more demanding classification task than that in (Mitchell et al., 2008) and describe their qualitative relationship to the features proposed in that paper.

1 Introduction

In the last few years there has been a gradual increase in the number of papers that resort to machine learning classifiers to decode information from the pattern of activation of activation of voxels across the brain (see (Norman et al., 2006) and (Haynes and Rees, 2006) for pointers to much of this work). Recently, however, interest has shifted to discovering how the information present is encoded, rather than just whether it is present, and also testing theories about that encoding. One especially compelling example of the latter is (Kay et al., 2008), where the authors postulate a mathematical model for how visual information gets transformed into the fMRI signal one can record from visual cortex and, after fitting the model, validate it by using it to predict fMRI

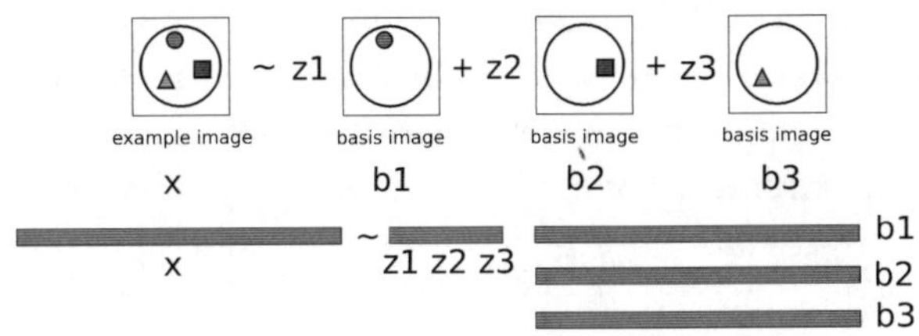

Figure 1: **top:** A complex pattern of activation is expressed as a combination of three basic patterns. **bottom:** The pattern can be written as a row vector, and the combination as a linear combination of three row vectors.

activation for novel stimuli. A second example is, of course, (Mitchell et al., 2008), which aims at decomposing the pattern of activation in response to a picture+noun stimulus into a combination of basic patterns corresponding to the key semantic features of the stimulus. A schematic view of this is given in Figure 1, where the complex pattern on the left is split into three simpler ones. This is done by determining the value of several hypothesized semantic features and using them as the combination weights for basic patterns, which can then be extracted from fMRI data.

Ideally, semantic features should reflect what is in a subject's mind when she thinks about a concrete concept, e.g. whether it is animate or inanimate, or an object versus something natural. It also seems reasonable to expect that the main semantic features would likely be shared by most people thinking about the same concept; talking to someone about a chair or table requires a common understanding of the characteristics of that concept. (Mitchell et al., 2008) proposed a method for capturing such common understanding, by considering 25

Proceedings of the NAACL HLT 2010 First Workshop on Computational Neurolinguistics, pages 1–9,

verbs [1] reflecting, in their words, "basic sensory and motor activities, actions performed on objects, and actions involving changes to spatial relationships". For each of the 60 nouns corresponding to the stimului shown, they counted the *co-occurrence* of the noun with each of the 25 verbs in a large text corpus, converting those 25 counts into normalized feature values (the 25-vector has length 1). The hypothesis subjacent to this procedure is that the 25 verbs are a good proxy for the main characteristics of a concept, and that their frequent co-occurrence with the corresponding noun in text means that many different sources (and people) have that association in mind when using the noun; in a nutshell, the association reflects common understanding of the meaning of the noun. The results in (Mitchell et al., 2008) are an extremely compelling demonstration that text corpora contain information useful for parsing brain activation into component patterns that reflect semantic features.

We would like to go beyond the analysis in (Mitchell et al., 2008) by considering that stipulating the semantic features to consider – via the verb proxy – may limit the information that can be extracted. The verbs were selected to capture a range of characteristics described above, but this does not guarantee that those will be all the ones that are relevant, even for concrete concepts. But how to identify characteristics beyond those that one could hypothesize in advance?

This paper describes an approach to identifying semantic features from a text corpus in an unsupervised manner, without the need to specify verbs or any other proxy for those features. The first aspect of the approach is the use of a text corpus that goes beyond merely containing occurrences of the words. We use a subset of Wikipedia [2], which we chose because articles are definitional in style and also edited by many people, ensuring that they will contain the essential shared knowledge pertaining to the subject of the article. The articles in the subset were chosen because they pertained to concrete or imageable concepts, and the methodology for deciding on this is described in Section 2.2.2. One property in particular of text defining a concept will be especially helpful here: in order to make its meaning precise, it has to touch on most related concepts. This means that we will still be resorting to co-ocurrence with our target nouns in order to identify semantic features, but not of a fixed set of verbs; rather, we are considering all possible related words.

The tool we will use to do so is latent Dirichlet allocation (LDA, (Blei et al., 2003)). This technique produces a generative probabilistic model of text corpora where each document (article) is viewed as a bag-of-words (i.e. only which words appear, and how often, matters) with each word being drawn from a finite mixture of an underlying set of *topics*, each of which is in turn a probability distribution over vocabulary words. We will use topics as our semantic features, with the proportions of each topic in the article for a given noun being the values of the features for that noun.

(Murphy et al., 2009) does something similar in flavour to this, by decomposing the patterns of cooccurrences in a text corpus between the 20000 most frequent nouns and 5000 most frequent verbs using SVD. This is used to identify 25 singular vectors which yield feature values across nouns.

2 Methods and Data

2.1 Data

We use the dataset from (Mitchell et al., 2008), which contains data from 9 subjects. For each subject there is a dataset of 360 examples - average fMRI volume around the peak of an experiment trial - comprising 6 replications (epochs) of each of 60 nouns as stimuli. The 60 nouns also belong to one of 12 semantic categories, hence there are two labels for classification tasks. We refer the reader to the original paper for more details about the specific categories and nouns chosen.

All of our classification experiments are done over 360 examples, rather than 60 average noun images, as we want to leverage having multiple instances of the same noun and use cross-validation. We also replicated the main experiment in (Mitchell et al., 2008), and for that we used the 60 average noun images, with their mean image subtracted from each of them.

[1] see, hear, listen, taste, smell, eat, touch, rub, lift, manipulate, run, push, fill, move, ride, say, fear, open, approach, near, enter, drive, wear, break and clean

[2] `http://en.wikipedia.org`

2.2 Semantic Features

The experiments described on the paper rely on using two different kinds of semantic features (low-dimensional representations of data) to decompose each example in constituent basis images; these two kinds are described blow.

2.2.1 Science Semantic Features (SSF)

These are the semantic features used in (Mitchell et al., 2008) to represent a given stimulus. They were obtained by considering co-occurrence counts of the noun naming each stimulus with each of 25 verbs in a text corpus, yielding a vector of 25 counts which was normalized to have unit length. The low-dimensional representation of the brain image for a given noun is thus a 25-dimensional vector. The left of Figure 2 shows the value of these features for the 60 nouns considered.

2.2.2 Wikipedia Semantic Features (WSF)

To obtain the Wikipedia semantic features we considered concepts rather than nouns, though we will use the latter terminology in the rest of the paper for consistency with (Mitchell et al., 2008). We started with the classical lists of words in (Paivio et al., 1968) and (Battig and Montague, 1969), as well as modern revisions/extensions (Clark and Paivio, 2004) and (Van Overschelde, 2004), and looked for words corresponding to concepts that were deemed concrete or imageable (be it because of their score in one of the norms or through editorial decision), identified the corresponding Wikipedia article titles (e.g. "airplane" is "Fixed-wing aircraft") and also compiled related articles which were linked to from these (e.g. "Aircraft cabin"). If there were words in the original lists with multiple meanings we included the articles for at least several of those meanings. Given the time available, we stopped the process with a list of 3500 concepts and their corresponding articles (a corpus we call the "Weekipedia"). We used Wikipedia Extractor [3] to remove any HTML or wiki formatting and annotations and processed the resulting text through the morphological analysis tool Morpha (Minnen et al., 2001) [4] to lemmatize all the words to their basic stems (e.g. "taste","tasted","taster" and "tastes" all become the same word).

The resulting text corpus was processed with topic modelling software to build several LDA models. The articles were converted to the required format, keeping only words that appeared in at least two articles, and words were also excluded resorting to a custom stopword list. We run the software varying the number of topics allowed from 10 to 60, in increments of 5, and allowing the software to estimate the α parameter. The α parameter influences the number of topics used for each example. For a given number of topics K, this yielded distributions over the vocabulary for each topic and one vector of topic probabilities per article/concept; this vector is the low-dimensional representation of the concept. Note also that, since the probabilities add up to 1, the presence of one semantic feature trades off with the presence of the others.

The middle and right of Figure 2 shows the value of these features for the 60 nouns considered in 25 and 50 topic models, respectively.

2.2.3 Relating semantic features to brain images

notation Each example corresponds to the average fMRI volume around the peak of a trial, accounting for haemodynamic delay. This 3D volume can be unfolded into a vector $\mathbf{x}$ with as many entries as voxels. A dataset is a $n \times m$ matrix X where row i is the example vector $\mathbf{x}_i$. Similarly to (Mitchell et al., 2008), each example $\mathbf{x}$ will be expressed as a linear combination of basis images $\mathbf{b_1}, \ldots, \mathbf{b_K}$ of the same dimensionality, with the weights given by the semantic feature vector $\mathbf{z} = [z_1, \ldots, z_K]$ (see Figure 1 for an illustration of this). The low-dimensional representation of X is a $n \times K$ matrix Z where row i is a semantic feature vector $\mathbf{z}_i$ and the corresponding basis images are a $K \times m$ matrix B, where row k corresponds to basis image $\mathbf{b}_k$.

learning and prediction Learning the basis images given X and Z (top part of Figure 4) can be decomposed into a set of independent regression prob-

[3] http://medialab.di.unipi.it/wiki/Wikipedia_extractor

[4] http://www.informatics.susx.ac.uk/research/groups/nlp/carroll/morph.html

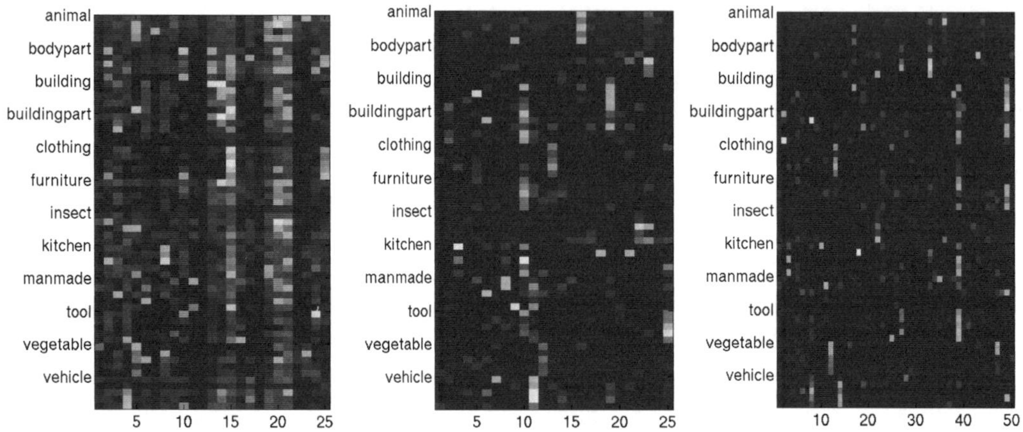

Figure 2: The value of semantic features for the 60 nouns considered, using SSF with 25 verbs (left) and WSF with 25 and 50 topics (middle and right). The 60 nouns belong to one of 12 categories, and those are arranged in sequence. Although a few of the SSF features might correspond to WSF features, the majority of them do not.

lems, one per voxel j, i.e. the values of voxel j across all examples, $X(:, j)$, are predicted from Z using regression coefficients $B(:, j)$, which are the values of voxel j across basis images.

Predicting the semantic feature vector $\mathbf{z}$ for an example $\mathbf{x}$ (bottom part of Figure 4) is a regression problem where $\mathbf{x}'$ is predicted from B' using regression coefficients $\mathbf{z}'$. For WSF, the prediction of the semantic feature vector is done under the additional constraint that the values need to add up to 1. Any situation where linear regression was unfeasible because the square matrix in the normal equations was not invertible was addressed by replacing the design matrix by its singular value decomposition, leaving only non-zero singular values.

3 Experiments and Discussion

3.1 Classification/Reconstruction on semantic feature space

3.1.1 Experiment details

Several classification experiments are described in (Mitchell et al., 2008). The main one aims at gauging the accuracy of matching unseen stimuli to their unseen fMRI images and is schematized in Figure 3. To do this, the authors consider the 60 average examples of each stimulus and, in turn, leave out each of 1770 possible pairs of examples. For each left out pair, they learn a set of basis images using the remaining 58 examples and their respective SSF representations. They then use the SSF representation of the two left-out examples and the basis to generate a *predicted example* for each one of them. These can then be used in a two-way matching task with the actual examples that were left out, where the outcome is correct or incorrect. Note that this is not done over the entire brain but over a selection of 500 stable voxels, as determined by computing their reproducibility over the 58 examples in each leave-one-out fold. This criterion identifies voxels whose activation levels across the 58 nouns bear the same relationship to each other over epochs (mathematically, the vector of activation levels across the 60 sorted nouns is highly correlated between epochs). We reproduced this experiment for the sake of comparison and describe the results in Section 3.4.

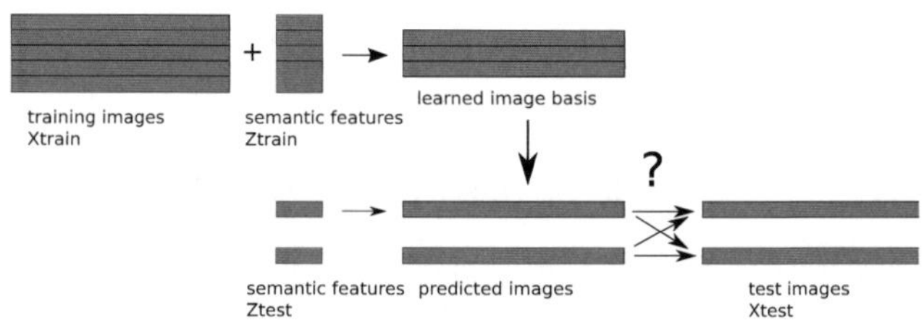

Figure 3: The classification task in (Mitchell et al., 2008) is such that semantic feature representations of the 2 test nouns are used, in conjunction with the image basis learned on the training set, to predict their respective test examples and use that prediction in a 2-way classification.

Whereas (Mitchell et al., 2008) aimed at predicting the activation of a set of voxels, and judging how

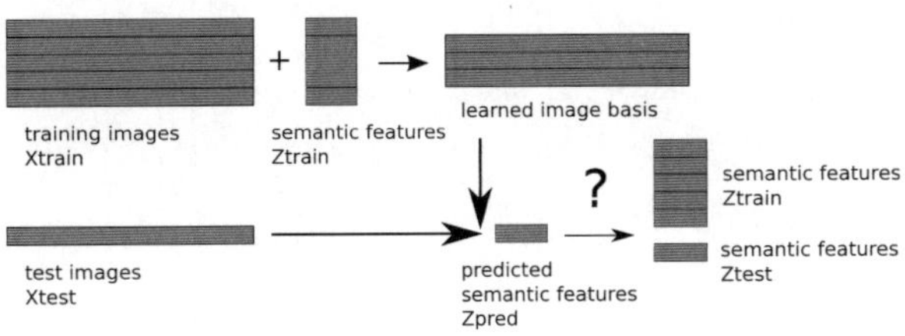

Figure 4: Our classification task requires learning an image basis from a set of training examples and their respective semantic feature representations. This is used to predict semantic feature values for test set examples and from those one can classify against the known semantic feature values for all 60 nouns.

good that prediction is by its 2-way accuracy, this paper focuses on a different sort of experiment: prediction of semantic feature values for a test example, as schematized in FIgure 4. In this experiment, the semantic features get used to learn basis images from training examples, with the goal of reconstructing those training examples as well as possible. This learning does not contemplate the labels – category or noun – of the training examples. The basis images are used, in turn, to predict semantic feature values for test examples and determining, in essence, which semantic features are active during a test example. The criterion for judging whether this is a good prediction will be how well can we classify the category (1-of-12) and noun (1-of-60) noun of a test example. Good classification performance implies that the semantic features capture activation that is relevant to the task in the corresponding basis images and that, in combination, the features contain enough information to distinguish the various nouns.

We will use either a leave-one-epoch-out (6 fold) or a leave-one-noun-out (60 fold) cross-validation and we perform the following steps in each fold:

1. from each training set X_{train} and corresponding semantic features Z_{train}, select the top 1000 most reproducible voxels and learn an image basis B using those
2. use the test set X_{test} and basis B to *predict* a semantic feature representation Z_{pred} for those examples
3. use nearest-neighbour classification to predict the labels of examples in X_{test}, by comparing Z_{pred} for each example with known semantic features Z
4. use the semantic features Z_{pred} together with basis B to reconstruct test examples as $X_{pred} = Z_{bred}B$ and compute squared error between X_{pred} and X_{test} (over selected voxels)

This allows us to do both kinds of cross-validation, as there is always one semantic feature vector for each different noun in Z regardless. This procedure is unbiased, and we tested this empirically using a permutation test (examples permuted within epoch) to verify the accuracy results for either task were at chance level.

3.1.2 Experiment results

Figure 5 shows the results using leave-one-epoch-out cross-validation. For each subject (row), there is one plot of reconstruction error (column 1) and one for error in category classification (column 2) and noun classification (column 3). Each plot contrasts the error obtained using SSF with that obtained using WSF with 10-60 topics, in increments of 5; WSF is as good or better than SSF in both category and noun classification. Given the the results are over 360 test examples we are not displaying error bars; each number of topics for which WSF is better as deemed by a paired t-test (0.01 significance level, uncorrected) is highlighted by a square on the plot. The same is true for the category task when using leave-one-noun-out cross-validation, but neither WSF nor SSF appear to do well in the noun task except for subject P1, where WSF again dominates. Results overall are somewhat lower than for the leave-one-epoch-out cross-validation. Given that the comparison results are qualitatively similar and space is limited we did not include the corresponding figure. In both cross-validations the reconstruction error of WSF starts higher than that of SSF and decreases monotonically until they are roughly matched. Our conjecture is that WSF semantic features are sparser and thus there are fewer basis images being added to predict any given test example. As the number of topics increases, this ceases to be the case.

One salient aspect of Figure 5 is that accuracy is much higher than chance for subjects P1-P4 than for P5-P9, and this corresponds to the subjects where

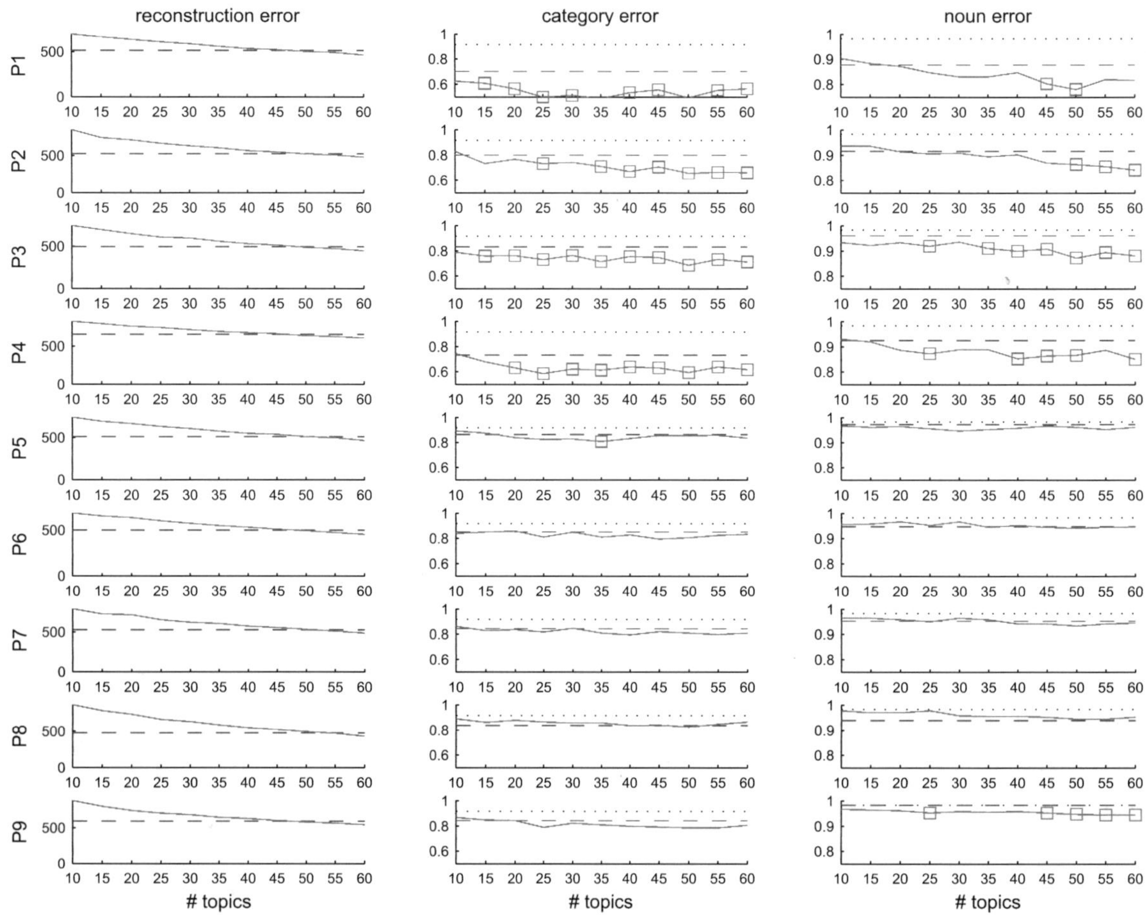

Figure 5: For each of the 9 subjects (rows) a comparison between SSF and WSF (using 10-60 topics) in reconstruction error (column 1) and classification error in the category (column 2) and noun (column 3) tasks. In each plot WSF is red (full line), SSF is blue (constant dashed line) and chance level is black (constant dotted line). The reconstruction error is measured on left out examples, over the 1000 voxels selected on the training set. These results were obtained using leave-one-epoch-out cross-validation (one epoch containing one instance of all nouns is left out in each of 6 folds). Error bars are not shown, given their small size (there are 360 examples), but each number of topics for which WSF error is significantly lower than SSF error is highlighted with a square.

	P1	P2	P3	P4	P5	P6	P7	P8	P9
same	0.57	0.39	0.36	0.32	0.26	0.16	0.26	0.24	0.18
category	0.50	0.32	0.30	0.28	0.24	0.14	0.23	0.21	0.16
other	0.45	0.30	0.27	0.22	0.22	0.13	0.21	0.20	0.14
same minus other	0.12	0.09	0.09	0.10	0.04	0.03	0.05	0.04	0.04
same minus category	0.07	0.07	0.06	0.04	0.02	0.02	0.03	0.03	0.02

Table 1: For each subject (column), the average correlation between one test example of a noun and all training set examples of the same noun (same), those which are not the same but belong to the same category (category) and those which are not in the same category (other). The correlation is computed over the 1000 voxels selected in the training set which are used to learn the image basis. Note the difference between same and other for subjects P1-P4, in contrast with that for subjects P5-P9. This was computed using leave-one-epoch-out cross-validation, and thus should be used in conjunction with Figure 5.

WSF is significantly better than SSF. In an effort to find out why this was the case, we computed a measure of *consistency* of the data from each of the subjects; intuitively, this is the degree to which the brain activation pattern was similar between trials with the same noun stimulus (and dissimilar for trials where the stimulus was different). This was computed in leave-one-epoch-out cross-validation, and consisted of examining the correlation – computed across selected voxels – of a test example with training examples of the same noun (same), the same category but a different noun (same category) and different category and noun (other); the measures were averaged across examples. In leave-one-group-out cross-validation subjects P1-P4 have higher differences between correlation within examples of a noun and examples in the same category or other categories than subjects P5-P9, which suggests that the former are more consistent in how they elicit patterns in response to the same stimulus.

3.2 Classification on voxel space

In order to have an idea of how much of the information present either SSF or WSF can extract and convey via their respective low-dimensional representations, we also trained a simple Gaussian Naive Bayes (GNB) classifier on voxels selected using the same reproducibility criterion described earlier. We used leave-one-epoch-out cross-validation and both category and noun tasks, respectively top and bottom of Table 2. Contrasting this with Figure 5, it's clear that the accuracies in the category task are comparable, whereas those in the noun task are somewhat lower; this suggests that either information about individual nouns is lost when converting from voxels to semantic features, or that nearest-neighbour is not the best classifier to use.

3.3 Similarity between SSF and WSF representations

In order to gauge the quality of the semantic feature representations we can consider both how much they differ between different nouns (and different categories) and also how consistent they are for the 6 examples of the same noun. This is shown for subject P1 in Figure 6, where the semantic feature vectors learned for 360 examples are correlated, for WSF 50 (left) and SSF 25 (right). Examples are sorted so that

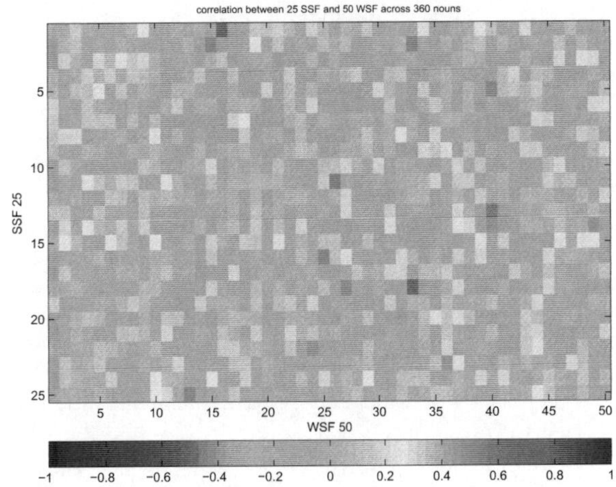

Figure 7: Correlation between each pair of SSF and WSF vectors of predicted feature values across 360 examples.

the 6 examples of the same noun are together, and adjacent to the other 24 belonging to the same category (and the category changes are labelled. Note that these are the values obtained when each example was in the test set, rather than the values derived from text for each noun; this is why the semantic feature vectors for the 6 examples of the same noun are different. WSF 50 is such that nouns belonging to the same category share many feature values, and hence show up as large blocks along the diagonal of the correlation matrix. Less of the noun specific information is being captured, but it is sometimes visible as the smaller blocks along the diagonal, inside the large blocks.

We can also consider the question of whether SSF and WSF representations are similar, i.e. whether a given SSF feature has values across examples similar to a given WSF feature. This can be done by considering the correlation between each pair of predicted SSF/WSF vectors across 360 examples, which is shown in Figure 7. This suggests very few of the semantic features are similar when predicted for examples in the test set, and as was already evidence in Figure 2.

3.4 Leave-2-out 2-way classification

We have also attempted to replicate the results in the main experiment in (Mitchell et al., 2008), schematized in Figure 3 and described earlier in Section 3.1.1. The results of this are shown in Table 3, which compares the mean accuracy across

category accuracy #voxels	100	250	500	1000	1500	2000	5000	all voxels
P1	0.43	0.53	0.54	0.56	0.53	0.52	0.42	0.08
P2	0.30	0.34	0.32	0.30	0.28	0.26	0.22	0.08
P3	0.25	0.27	0.29	0.27	0.26	0.26	0.21	0.08
P4	0.42	0.40	0.41	0.38	0.38	0.39	0.31	0.08
P5	0.20	0.21	0.21	0.17	0.16	0.14	0.11	0.08
P6	0.27	0.23	0.19	0.16	0.14	0.13	0.10	0.08
P7	0.21	0.19	0.19	0.19	0.18	0.16	0.13	0.08
P8	0.14	0.13	0.12	0.14	0.13	0.13	0.12	0.08
P9	0.18	0.21	0.21	0.21	0.22	0.21	0.19	0.08
noun accuracy #voxels	100	250	500	1000	1500	2000	5000	all voxels
P1	0.34	0.41	0.41	0.41	0.35	0.33	0.23	0.02
P2	0.26	0.32	0.29	0.22	0.18	0.17	0.08	0.02
P3	0.17	0.20	0.21	0.17	0.14	0.12	0.07	0.02
P4	0.21	0.23	0.22	0.20	0.18	0.16	0.14	0.02
P5	0.11	0.09	0.08	0.06	0.05	0.05	0.03	0.02
P6	0.13	0.08	0.06	0.04	0.04	0.04	0.02	0.02
P7	0.08	0.07	0.08	0.07	0.07	0.07	0.05	0.02
P8	0.07	0.08	0.06	0.05	0.05	0.04	0.03	0.02
P9	0.06	0.08	0.06	0.06	0.05	0.05	0.04	0.02

Table 2: **top:** Accuracy of a Gaussian Naive Bayes classifier trained on various numbers of voxels selected by the reproducibility criterion, on the category prediction task, using leave-one-epoch-out cross-validation. **bottom:** Same, for the noun prediction task.

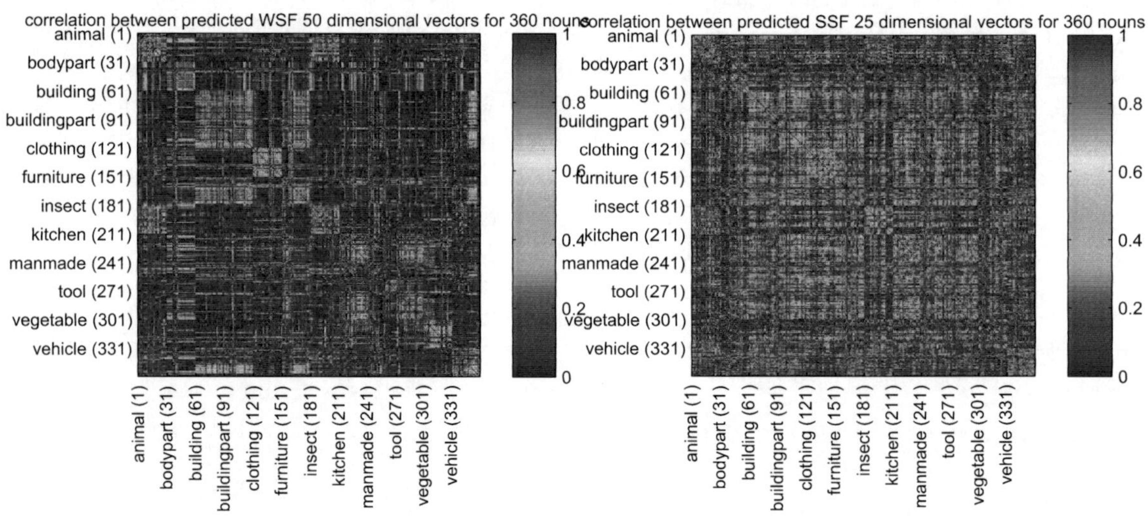

Figure 6: **left:** correlation between the WSF 50 predicted feature vectors for the 360 examples **right:** same for the SSF 25 predicted feature vectors

	SSF	Org	20	25	30	35	40	45	50
P1	0.84	0.83	0.88	0.91	0.87	0.89	0.85	0.85	0.86
P2	0.80	0.76	0.75	0.77	0.74	0.76	0.72	0.72	0.73
P3	0.78	0.78	0.76	0.78	0.73	0.76	0.72	0.70	0.78
P4	0.82	0.72	0.88	0.88	0.85	0.86	0.86	0.85	0.87
P5	0.85	0.78	0.79	0.84	0.78	0.71	0.78	0.73	0.78
P6	0.77	0.85	0.82	0.84	0.78	0.79	0.76	0.81	0.75
P7	0.78	0.73	0.83	0.84	0.80	0.81	0.79	0.75	0.74
P8	0.77	0.68	0.66	0.68	0.64	0.62	0.67	0.64	0.69
P9	0.75	0.82	0.77	0.81	0.77	0.79	0.81	0.78	0.78

Table 3: Results of a replication of the leave-2-noun-out 2-way classification experiment in (Mitchell et al., 2008). For subjects P1-P9, SSF represents the mean accuracy obtained using SSF (across 1770 leave-2-out pairs), Org the mean accuracy reported in (Mitchell et al., 2008) and the remaining columns the mean accuracy obtained using WSF with 20-50 topics.

1770 leave-2-out pairs using SSF, the mean accuracy reported in (Mitchell et al., 2008) and the mean accuracy using WSF with 20-50 topics. We were not able to exactly reproduce the numbers in (Mitchell et al., 2008), despite the same data preprocessing (making each example mean 0 and standard deviation 1, prior to averaging all the repetitions of each noun, and then subtracting the mean of all average examples from each one), the same voxel selection procedure (using 500 voxels) and the same ridge regression function (although (Mitchell et al., 2008) does not mention the value of the ridge parameter λ, which we assumed to be 1). We will endeavour to identify the source of the discrepancies, but it was not possible to do so in time for this paper.

4 Conclusions

We have shown that it is feasible to learn semantic features from a text corpus, without the need to postulate what they might represent in the brain, either directly or via proxy indicators like the verbs in (Mitchell et al., 2008). Furthermore, we have shown that those semantic features are superior to the features proposed in (Mitchell et al., 2008) in two demanding classification tasks that require using the features to decompose brain activation into basis images related to them. Further analysis of those and other results obtained classifying directly from voxels suggest that the semantic features capture a large amount of category-level information, and at least a fraction of the noun-level information present in the pattern of brain activation. (Mitchell et al., 2008).

Acknowledgments

We would like to thank David Blei for discussions about topic modelling in general and of the Wikipedia corpus in particular and Ken Norman for valuable feedback at various stages of the work.

References

William F Battig and William E Montague. 1969. Category Norms for Verbal Items in 56 Categories. *Journal of Experimental Psychology*, 80(3).

D M Blei, A Y Ng, and M I Jordan. 2003. Latent Dirichlet allocation. *Journal of Machine Learning Research*, 3:993–1022.

James M Clark and Allan Paivio. 2004. Extensions of the Paivio, Yuille, and Madigan (1968) norms. *Behavior research methods, instruments, & computers : a journal of the Psychonomic Society, Inc*, 36(3):371–83, August.

John-Dylan Haynes and Geraint Rees. 2006. Decoding mental states from brain activity in humans. *Nature reviews. Neuroscience*, 7(7):523–34.

Kendrick N Kay, Thomas Naselaris, Ryan J Prenger, and Jack L Gallant. 2008. Identifying natural images from human brain activity. *Nature*, 452(7185):352–5.

G. Minnen, J. Carroll, and D. Pearce. 2001. Applied morphological processing of English. *Natural Language Engineering*, 7(03):207223.

Tom M Mitchell, Svetlana V Shinkareva, Andrew Carlson, Kai-Min Chang, Vicente L Malave, Robert a Mason, and Marcel Adam Just. 2008. Predicting human brain activity associated with the meanings of nouns. *Science (New York, N.Y.)*, 320(5880):1191–5.

B. Murphy, M. Baroni, and M. Poesio. 2009. EEG Responds to Conceptual Stimuli and Corpus Semantics. *Proceedings of ACL/EMNLP*.

Kenneth A Norman, Sean M Polyn, Greg J Detre, and James V Haxby. 2006. Beyond mind-reading: multi-voxel pattern analysis of fMRI data. *Trends in cognitive sciences*, 10(9):424–30.

Allan Paivio, John C Yuille, and Stephen A Madigan. 1968. Concreteness, Imagery, and Meaningfulness Values for 925 Nouns. *Journal of Experimental Psychology*, 76(1).

J Van Overschelde. 2004. Category norms: An updated and expanded version of the Battig and Montague (1969) norms. *Journal of Memory and Language*, 50(3):289–335.

Concept Classification with Bayesian Multi-task Learning

Marcel van Gerven
Radboud University Nijmegen
Intelligent Systems
Heyendaalseweg 135 6525 AJ
Nijmegen, The Netherlands
marcelge@cs.ru.nl

Irina Simanova
Max Planck Institute for Psycholinguistics
Wundtlaan 1 6525 XD
Nijmegen, The Netherlands
irina.simanova@mpi.nl

Abstract

Multivariate analysis allows decoding of single trial data in individual subjects. Since different models are obtained for each subject it becomes hard to perform an analysis on the group level. We introduce a new algorithm for Bayesian multi-task learning which imposes a coupling between single-subject models. Using the CMU fMRI dataset it is shown that the algorithm can be used for concept classification based on the average activation of regions in the AAL atlas. Concepts which were most easily classified correspond to the categories shelter, manipulation and eating, which is in accordance with the literature. The multi-task learning algorithm is shown to find regions of interest that are common to all subjects which therefore facilitates interpretation of the obtained models.

1 Introduction

Multivariate analysis allows decoding of neural representations at the single trial level in single subjects. Its introduction into the field of cognitive neuroscience has led to novel insights about the neural representation of cognitive functions such as language (Mitchell et al., 2008), memory (Hassabis et al., 2009), and vision (Miyawaki et al., 2008).

However, interpretation of the models obtained using a multivariate analysis can be hard due to the fact that different models are obtained for individual subjects. For example, when analyzing K separately acquired datasets, K sets of model parameters will be obtained which may or may not show a common pattern. In some sense, we are in need of a second-level analysis such that we can draw inferences on the group level, as in the conventional analysis of neuroimaging data using the general linear model. One way to achieve this in the context of multivariate analysis is by means of multi-task learning, a special case of transfer learning (Thrun, 1996) where model parameters for different tasks (datasets) are estimated simultaneously and no longer assumed to be independent (Caruana, 1997). In an fMRI context, multi-task learning has been explored using canonical correlation analysis (Rustandi et al., 2009).

In a Bayesian setting, multi-task learning is typically realized by assuming a hierarchical Bayesian framework where shared prior distributions condition task-specific parameters (Gelman et al., 1995). In this paper, we explore a new Bayesian approach to multi-task learning in the context of concept classification; i.e., the prediction of the semantic category of concrete nouns from BOLD response. Effectively, we are using a shared prior to induce parameter shrinkage. We show that Bayesian multi-task learning leads to more interpretable models, thereby facilitating the interpretation of the models obtained using multivariate analysis.

2 Bayesian multi-task learning

The goal of concept classification is to predict the semantic category y of a presented (and previously unseen) concrete noun from the measured BOLD response $\mathbf{x}$. In this paper, we will use Bayesian logistic regression as the underlying classification model. Let $\mathcal{B}(y; p) = p^y(1-p)^{1-y}$ denote the Bernoulli distribution and $l(x) = \log(x/(1-x))$ the logit link

Proceedings of the NAACL HLT 2010 First Workshop on Computational Neurolinguistics, pages 10–17,
Los Angeles, California, June 2010.

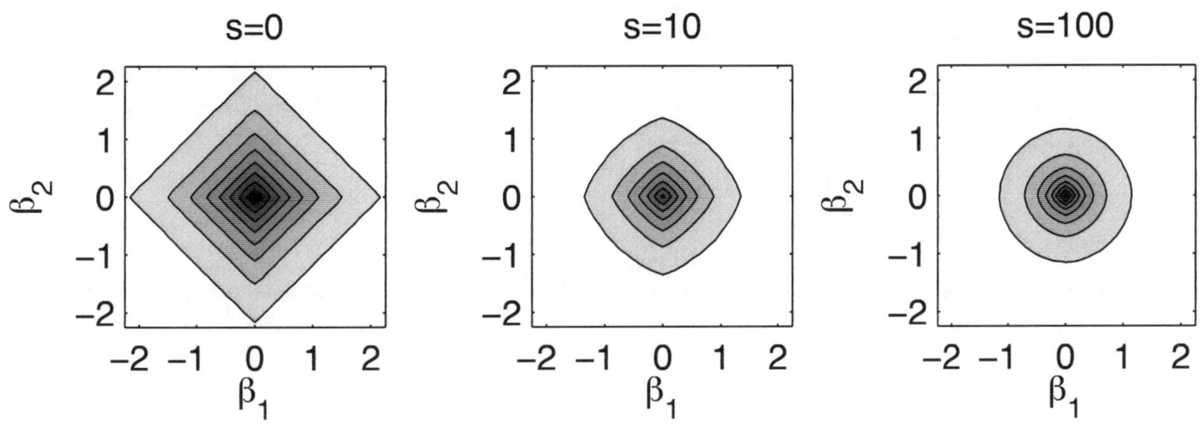

Figure 1: Contour plots of samples drawn from the prior for two regression coefficients β_1 and β_2 given three different values of the coupling strength s. For uncoupled covariates, the magnitude of one covariate has no influence on the magnitude of the other covariate. For strongly coupled covariates, in contrast, a large magnitude of one covariate increases the probability of a large magnitude in the other covariate.

function. We are interested in the following predictive density:

$$p(y \mid \mathbf{x}, \mathbf{D}, \boldsymbol{\Theta}) = \int \mathcal{B}(y; l^{-1}(\mathbf{x}^T\boldsymbol{\beta}))p(\boldsymbol{\beta} \mid \mathbf{D}, \boldsymbol{\Theta})d\boldsymbol{\beta}$$

where we integrate out the regression coefficients $\boldsymbol{\beta}$ and condition on the response $\mathbf{x}$, observed training data $\mathbf{D} = (\mathbf{y}, \mathbf{X})$ and hyper-parameters $\boldsymbol{\Theta}$. Using Bayes rule, we can write the second term on the right hand side as

$$p(\boldsymbol{\beta} \mid \mathbf{D}, \boldsymbol{\Theta}) \propto p(\mathbf{D} \mid \boldsymbol{\beta})p(\boldsymbol{\beta} \mid \boldsymbol{\Theta}) \qquad (1)$$

where

$$p(\mathbf{D} \mid \boldsymbol{\beta}) = \prod_n \mathcal{B}(y_n; l^{-1}(\mathbf{x}_n^T\boldsymbol{\beta}))$$

is the likelihood term, which does not depend on the hyper-parameters $\boldsymbol{\Theta}$, and $p(\boldsymbol{\beta} \mid \boldsymbol{\Theta})$ is the prior on the regression coefficients.

Let $\mathcal{N}(\mathbf{x}; \boldsymbol{\mu}, \boldsymbol{\Theta})$ denote a multivariate Gaussian with mean $\boldsymbol{\mu}$ and covariance matrix $\boldsymbol{\Theta}$. In order to couple the tasks in a multi-task problem, we will use the multivariate Laplace prior, which can be written as a scale-mixture using auxiliary variables $\mathbf{u}$ and $\mathbf{v}$ (van Gerven et al., 2010):

$$p(\boldsymbol{\beta} \mid \boldsymbol{\Theta}) = \int \left(\prod_k \mathcal{N}(\beta_k; 0, u_k^2 + v_k^2) \right) \times \mathcal{N}(\mathbf{u}; \mathbf{0}, \boldsymbol{\Theta})\mathcal{N}(\mathbf{v}; \mathbf{0}, \boldsymbol{\Theta})d\mathbf{u}\, d\mathbf{v}$$

The multivariate Laplace prior allows one to control the prior variance of the regression coefficients $\boldsymbol{\beta}$ through the covariance matrix $\boldsymbol{\Theta}$ of the auxiliary variables $\mathbf{u}$ and $\mathbf{v}$. This covariance matrix is conveniently specified in terms of the precision matrix:

$$\boldsymbol{\Theta}^{-1} = \frac{1}{\theta}\mathbf{VRV}.$$

Here, θ is a scale parameter which controls regularization of the regression coefficients towards zero and $\mathbf{R}$ is a structure matrix where $r_{ij} = -s$ specifies a fixed coupling strength s between covariate i and covariate j. A negative r_{ij} penalizes differences between covariates i and j, see van Gerven et al. (2010) for details. $\mathbf{V}$ is a scaling matrix whose sole purpose is to ensure that the prior variance of the auxiliary variables is independent of the coupling strength.[1] Figure 1 shows the multivariate Laplace prior for two covariates and three different coupling strengths.

The specification of the prior in terms of θ and $\mathbf{R}$ promotes sparse solutions and allows the inclusion of prior knowledge about the relation between covariates. The posterior marginals for the latent variables $(\boldsymbol{\beta}, \mathbf{u}, \mathbf{v})$ can be approximated using expectation propagation (Minka, 2001) and the posterior variance of the auxiliary variables u_i (or v_i by symmetry) can be interpreted as a measure of im-

[1] $\mathbf{V}$ is a matrix with $\sqrt{\text{diag}(\mathbf{R}^{-1})}$ on the diagonal.

portance of the corresponding covariate x_i since it eventually determines how large the regression coefficients β_i can become.

Interpretation becomes complicated whenever we have collected multiple datasets for the same task since each corresponding model may give different results regarding the importance of the covariates used when solving the classification problem. Multi-task learning presents a solution to this problem by dropping the assumption that datasets $\{\mathbf{D}_1, \ldots, \mathbf{D}_K\}$ are independent. Here, this is easily realized using the multivariate Laplace prior by working with the augmented dataset

$$\mathbf{D}^* = \left(\begin{bmatrix} \mathbf{y}_1 \\ \mathbf{y}_2 \\ \vdots \\ \mathbf{y}_K \end{bmatrix}, \begin{bmatrix} \mathbf{X}_1 & \mathbf{0} & \mathbf{0} & \mathbf{0} \\ \mathbf{0} & \mathbf{X}_2 & \mathbf{0} & \mathbf{0} \\ \mathbf{0} & \mathbf{0} & \ddots & \mathbf{0} \\ \mathbf{0} & \mathbf{0} & \mathbf{0} & \mathbf{X}_K \end{bmatrix} \right)$$

and by assuming that each covariate is coupled between datasets. I.e., the structure matrix is given by elements

$$r_{ij} = \begin{cases} -s & \text{if } i \neq j \text{ and} \\ & (i-j) \bmod P = 0 \\ 1 + (K-1) \cdot s & \text{if } i = j \\ 0 & \text{otherwise} \end{cases}$$

where P stands for the number of covariates in each dataset. In this way, we have coupled covariates over datasets with coupling strength s. Note that this coupling is realized on the level of the auxiliary variables and not on the regression coefficients. Hence, coupled auxiliary variables control the magnitude of the regression coefficients $\boldsymbol{\beta}$ but the $\boldsymbol{\beta}$'s themselves can still be different for the individual subjects.

3 Experiments

In order to test our approach to Bayesian multi-task learning for concept classification we have made use of the CMU fMRI dataset[2], which consists of sixty concrete concepts in twelve categories. The dataset was collected while nine English speakers were presented with sixty line drawings of objects with text labels and were instructed to think of the same properties of the stimulus object consistently during each presentation. For each concept there are six instances per subject for which BOLD response in multiple voxels was measured.

In our experiments we assessed whether previously unseen concepts from two different categories (e.g., *building-tool*) can be classified correctly based on measured BOLD response. To this end, all concepts belonging to two out of the twelve semantic categories were selected. Subsequently, we trained a classifier on all concepts belonging to these two categories save one. The semantic category of the six instances of the left-out concept were then predicted using the trained classifier. This procedure was repeated for each of the concepts and classification performance was averaged over all concepts. This performance was computed for all of the 66 possible category pairs.

In order to determine the effect of multi-task learning, results were obtained when assuming no coupling between datasets ($s = 0$) as well as when assuming a very strong coupling between datasets ($s = 100$). The scale parameter was fixed to $\theta = 1$. In order to allow the coupling to be made, all datasets are required to contain the same features. One way to achieve this is to warp the data for each subject from native space to normalized space and to perform the multi-task learning in normalized space. Here, in contrast, we computed the average activation in 116 predefined regions of interest (ROIs) using the AAL atlas (Tzourio-Mazoyer et al., 2002). ROI activations were used as input to the classifier. This considerably reduces computational overhead since we need to couple just 116 ROIs instead of approximately 20000 voxels between all nine subjects.[3] Furthermore, it facilitates interpretation since results can be analyzed at the ROI level instead of at the single voxel level. Of course, this presupposes that category-specific information is captured by the average activation in predefined ROIs, which is an important open question we set out to answer with our experiments.

4 Results

4.1 Classification of category pairs

We achieved good classification performance for many of the category pairs both with and with-

[2]http://www.cs.cmu.edu/~tom/science2008

[3]The efficiency of our algorithm depends on the sparseness of the structure matrix $\mathbf{R}$.

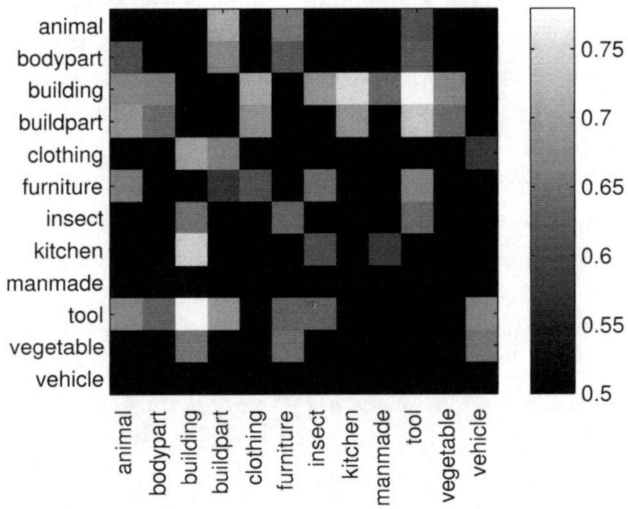

Figure 2: Accuracies for concept classification of the 66 category pairs. The upper triangular part shows the results of multi-task learning whereas the lower triangular part shows the results of standard classification. Non-significant outcomes have been masked (Wilcoxon rank sum test on outcomes for all nine subjects, p=0.05, Bonferroni corrected).

out multi-task learning. Figure 2 shows these results where non-significant outcomes have been masked. Interestingly, outcomes for all subjects showed a preference for particular category pairs. The concepts from *building-tool*, *building-kitchen* and *buildpart-tool* had the highest mean classification accuracies (proportion of correctly classifier trials) of 0.78, 0.76 and 0.74, closely followed by concepts from *building-clothing* and *animal-buildpart* with a mean classification accuracy of 0.71.

This result bears a strong resemblance to the recent work of Just et al. (2010). The authors conducted a factor analysis of fMRI brain activation in response to presentations of written words of different categories and discovered three semantic factors with the highest predictive potential: manipulation, eating and shelter-entry. They subsequently used these factors to select voxels for a features set and were able to accurately identify the activation generated by concrete word using multivariate learning methods on the basis of selected voxels. Moreover, using the factor-related activation profiles they were able to identify common neuronal signatures for particular words across participants. The authors suggest the revealed factors to represent major semantic dimensions that relate to the ways the human being can interact with an object. Although they assume the existence of other semantic attributes that determine conceptual representation, the factors shelter, manipulation and eating are proposed to be dominant for the particular set of nouns. It is easy to draw an analogy as the set of words used by Just and colleagues was exactly the same as in the current study. Although the taxonomic categorization used in our study does not exactly match the factor-based categorization, most of the items from categories *building*, *buildpart*, *tool* and *kitchen* show a strong correspondence with one of the semantic factors and are listed among ten words with highest factor scores according to Just et al. (2010) (see Table 1).

Table 1: Stimulus words from the semantic categories that showed best classification accuracies. Superscripts indicate the words belonging to the list of ten words with highest factor scores in the study by Just et al. (Just, 2010). We use the following abbreviations: s = shelter, m = manipulation, e = eating.

Building	Buildpart	Tool	Kitchen
apartment^{s}	window	chisel^{m}	glass^{e}
barn	door^{s}	hammer^{m}	knife^{m}
house^{s}	chimney	screwdriver^{m}	bottle
church^{s}	closet^{s}	pliers^{m}	cup^{e}
igloo	arch	saw^{m}	spoon^{m}

The subsets of items that are set far apart in the suggested semantic dimensions appear to be preferred by the classifier in our study. The classifier was not able to identify the category of an unseen concept in pairs *building-buildpart* and *tool-kitchen*, possibly since they these categories shared the same semantic features. Thus, the current study brings an independent corroboration for the finding on the semantic dimensions underlying concrete noun representation.

4.2 Single versus multi-task learning

The use of AAL regions instead of native voxel activity patterns allowed efficient multi-task learning by coupling each region between nine subjects. Reliable classification accuracies were obtained for all the participants, although there were strong differences in individual performances (Fig. 3). The move

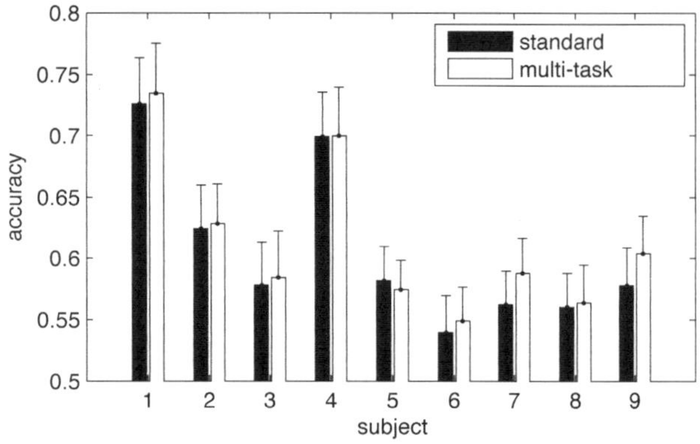

Figure 3: Classification performance per subject averaged over all category pairs for standard classification and multi-task learning (error bars show standard error of the mean).

to multi-task learning seems to improve classification results slightly in most of subjects, although the improvement is not significant.

The main outcome and advantage of our approach to multi-task learning is the convergence of models obtained from different subjects. Figure 4 shows that the subject-specific models become strongly correlated when they are obtained in the multi-task setting, even for weak coupling strengths. For strong coupling strengths, the models are almost perfectly correlated, resulting in identical models for all the nine subjects as shown in Fig. 4 for the category pair *building-tool*. It is important to realize here that the model is defined in terms of the variance of the auxiliary variables, which acts as a proxy to the importance of a region. At the level of the regression coefficients β, the model will still find subject-specific parameters due to the likelihood term in Eq. (1). Even though the contribution of each brain region is constrained by the induced coupling, this does not impede but rather improve classification performance. This fact entitles us to believe that our approach to multi-task learning tracks down the common task-specific activations while ignoring background noise.

Our study demonstrates that Bayesian multi-task learning allows generalization across subjects. Our algorithm identifies identical cortical locations as being important in solving the classification problem for all individuals within the group. The identified regions agree with previously published results on concept encoding. For example, the regions which were considered important for the category pair *building-tool* (Fig. 5) are almost indistinguishable from those described in a recent study by Shinkareva et al. (2008). These are regions that are traditionally considered to be involved in reading, objects meaning retrieval and visual semantic tasks (Vandenberghe et al., 1996; Phillips et al., 2002).

Strikingly, very similar regions were picked by the classifier for the other two category pairs with high classification accuracy, i.e., *building-kitchen* and *buildpart-tool*. This fact brings back the issue about the semantic factors relevant for the discrimination of the entities from these categories. The factors shelter, manipulation and eating are associated with the concepts from the first three addressed category pairs. The locations of voxel clusters associated with the semantic factors in (Just et al., 2010) match the brain regions that contributed to the classification for the three most optimal pairs in our experiment. In the Just et al. study these were left and right fusiform gyri, left and right precuneus and left inferior temporal gyrus for shelter, left supramarginal gyrus, left postcentral gyrus and left inferior temporal gyrus for manipulation and left inferior frontal gyrus, left middle/inferior frontal gyri, and left inferior temporal gyrus for eating. The occipital lobes detected exclusively in our experiment might be explained by the fact that in our experiment the subjects were viewing picture-text pairs in contrast to only text in (Just et al., 2010).

5 Discussion

We have demonstrated that Bayesian multi-task learning can be realized through Bayesian logistic regression when using a multivariate Laplace prior that couples features between multiple datasets. This approach has not been used before and yields promising results. As such it complements other Bayesian and non-Bayesian approaches to multi-task learning such as those reported in (Yu et al., 2005; Dunson et al., 2008; Argyriou et al., 2008; van Gerven et al., 2009; Obozinski et al., 2009; Rustandi et al., 2009).

Results show that many category pairs can be classified based on the average activation of regions

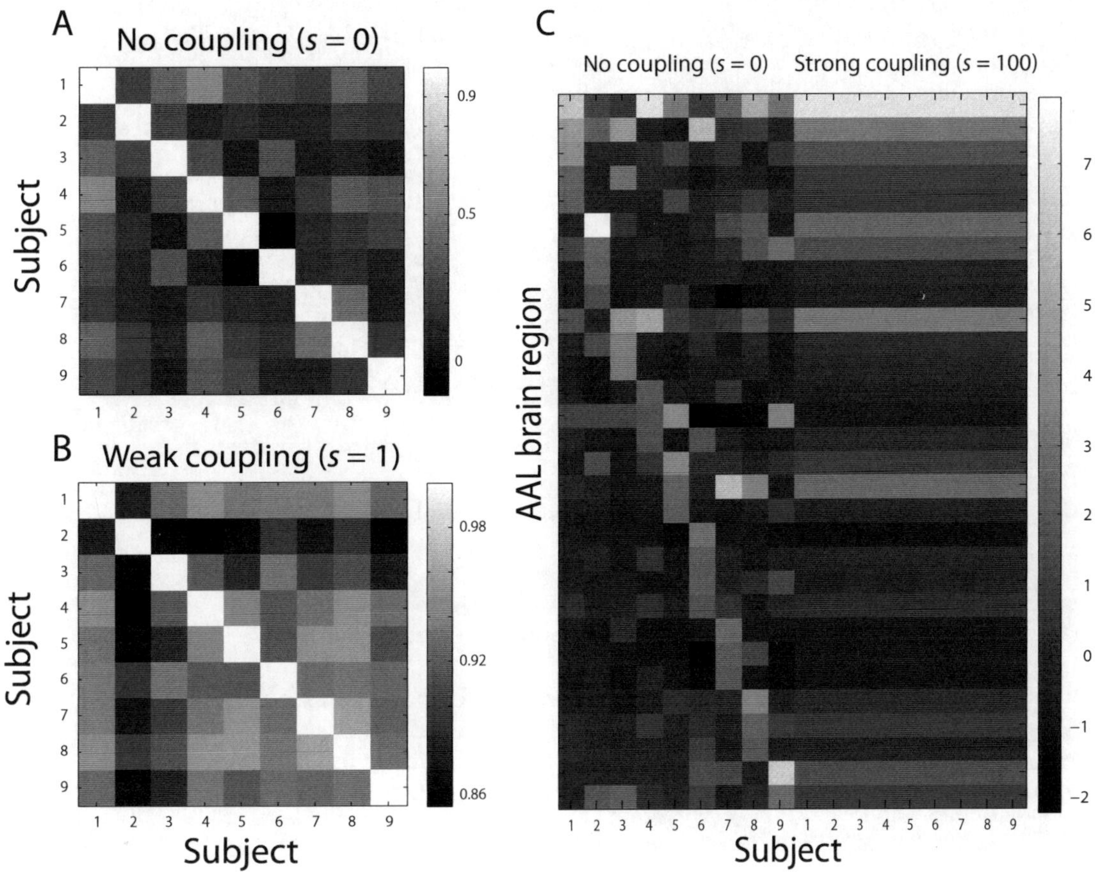

Figure 4: Correlation matrices for subject-specific models for standard classification (A) and multi-task learning (B) with weak coupling (s=1) for *building* versus *tool*. The right panel (C) shows the difference between the obtained models for standard classification and strong coupling (s=100) for the thirty most important AAL regions.

in the AAL template. Although obtained accuracies are lower than those which would have been obtained using single-voxel activations, it is interesting in its own right that the activation in just 116 predefined regions still allows concept decoding. However, it remains an open question to what extent classifiability truly reflects semantic processing instead of sensory processing of words and/or pictures.

The coupling induced by multi-task learning leads to interpretable models when using auxiliary variable variance as a measure of importance. The obtained models for the pairs which were easiest to classify corresponded well to the results reported in (Shinkareva et al., 2008) and mapped nicely onto the semantic features *shelter*, *manipulation* and *eating* identified in (Just et al., 2010).

In this paper we used the multivariate Laplace prior to induce a coupling between tasks. It is straightforward to combine this with other coupling constraints such as coupling nearby regions within subjects. Our algorithm also does not preclude multi-task learning on thousands of voxels. Computation time depends on the number of non-zeros in the structure matrix $\mathbf{R}$ and matrices containing hundreds of thousands of non-zero elements are still manageable with computation time being in the order of hours.

Another interesting application of multi-task learning in the context of concept learning is to couple the datasets of all condition pairs within a subject. This effectively tries to find a model where used regions of interest can predict multiple condition pairs. The correlation structure between the models for each condition pair then informs about their sim-

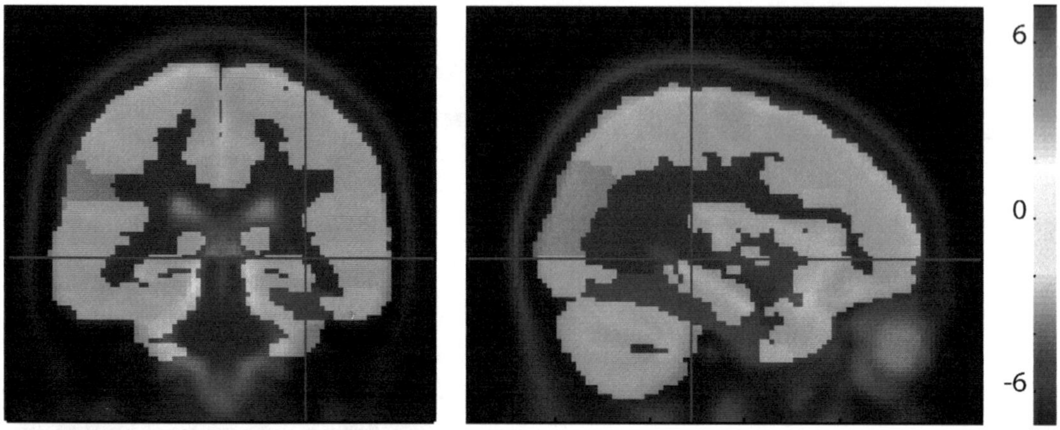

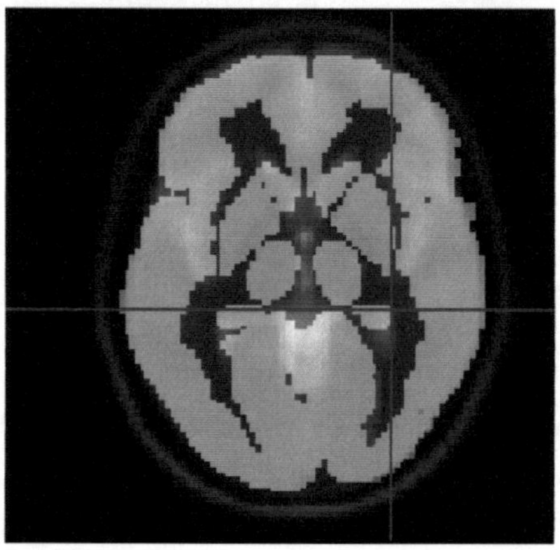

x = 36; y = -32; z = 2

Region	Z-score
R Fusiform gyrus	7.198
L Supramarginal gyrus	3.490
R Middle Occipital gyrus	3.191
L Superior Occipital gyrus	2.841
R Cuneus	2.593
R Inferior Temporal gyrus	1.701
L Cerebellum lobe 4-5	1.682
R Inferior Frontal gyrus (Pars triangularis)	1.526
L Postcentral gyrus	0.924
R Cerebellum lobe 4-5	0.901

Figure 5: The brain regions contributing to the identification of *building* versus *tool* categories.

ilarity. An interesting direction for future research is to perform multi-task learning on the level of the semantic features that define a concept instead of on the concepts themselves. If we are able to predict the semantic features reliably then we may be able to predict previously unseen concepts from their constituent features (Palatucci et al., 2009).

References

A. Argyriou, T Evgeniou, and M. Pontil. 2008. Convex multi-task feature learning. *Machine Learning*, 73(3):243–272.

R. Caruana. 1997. Multitask learning. *Machine Learning*, 28(1):41–75.

D. Dunson, Y. Xue, and L. Carin. 2008. The matrix stick-breaking process: flexible Bayes meta analysis. *Journal of the American Statistical Association*, 103(481):317–327.

A. Gelman, J. B. Carlin, H. S. Stern, and D. B. Rubin. 1995. *Bayesian Data Analysis*. Chapman and Hall, London, UK, 1st edition.

D. Hassabis, C. Chu, G. Rees, N. Weiskopf, P. D. Molyneux, and E. A. Maguire. 2009. Decoding neuronal ensembles in the human hippocampus. *Current Biology*, 19:546–554.

M. A. Just, V. L. Cherkassky, S. Aryal, and T. M. Mitchell. 2010. A neurosemantic theory of concrete noun representation based on the underlying brain codes. *PLoS ONE*, 5(1):e8622.

T. Minka. 2001. Expectation propagation for approximate Bayesian inference. In J. Breese and D. Koller, editors, *Proceedings of the Seventeenth Conference on Uncertainty in Artificial Intelligence*, pages 362–369. Morgan Kaufmann.

T. M. Mitchell, S. V. Shinkareva, A. Carlson, K.-M. Chang, V. L. Malave, R. A. Mason, and M. A. Just. 2008. Predicting human brain activity associated with the meanings of nouns. *Science*, 320(5880):1191–1195.

Y. Miyawaki, H. Uchida, O. Yamashita, M. Sato, Y. Morito, H. C. Tanabe, N. Sadato, and Y. Kamitani.

2008. Visual image reconstruction from human brain activity using a combination of multiscale local image decoders. *Neuron*, 60(5):915–929.

G. Obozinski, B. Taskar, and M. I. Jordan. 2009. Joint covariate selection and joint subspace selection for multiple classification problems. In *Statistics and Computing*. Springer.

M. Palatucci, D. Pomerleau, G. Hinton, and T. Mitchell. 2009. Zero-shot learning with semantic output codes. In Y. Bengio, D. Schuurmans, J. Lafferty, C. K. I. Williams, and A. Culotta, editors, *Neural Information Processing Systems*, pages 1410–1418.

J. A. Phillips, U. Noppeney, G. W. Humphreys, and C. J. Price. 2002. Can segregation within the semantic system account for category-specific deficits? *Brain*, 125(9):2067–2080.

I. Rustandi, M. A. Just, and T. M. Mitchell. 2009. Integrating multiple-study multiple-subject fMRI datasets using canonical correlation analysis. In *Proceedings of the MICCAI 2009 Workshop*.

S. V. Shinkareva, R. A. Mason, V. L. Malave, W. Wang, and T. M. Mitchell. 2008. Using fMRI brain activation to identify cognitive states associated with perception of tools and dwellings. *PLoS ONE*, 3(1):e1394.

S. Thrun. 1996. Is learning the n-th thing any easier than learning the first? In *Advances in Neural Information Processing Systems*, pages 640–646. The MIT Press.

N. Tzourio-Mazoyer, B. Landeau, D. Papathanassiou, F. Crivello, O. Etard, N. Delcroix, B. Mazoyer, and M. Joliot. 2002. Automated anatomical labeling of activations in SPM using a macroscopic anatomical parcellation of the MNI MRI single-subject brain. *Neuroimage*, 15(1):273–289.

M. A. J. van Gerven, C. Hesse, O. Jensen, and T. Heskes. 2009. Interpreting single trial data using groupwise regularisation. *NeuroImage*, 46:665–676.

M. A. J. van Gerven, B. Cseke, F. P. de Lange, and T. Heskes. 2010. Efficient Bayesian multivariate fMRI analysis using a sparsifying spatio-temporal prior. *NeuroImage*, 50(1):150–161.

R. Vandenberghe, C. Price, R. Wise, O. Josephs, and R. S. Frackowiak. 1996. Functional anatomy of a common semantic system for words and pictures. *Nature*, 383(6597):254–256.

K. Yu, V. Tresp, and A. Schwaighofer. 2005. Learning Gaussian processes from multiple tasks. In *International Conference on Machine Learning*, pages 1012–1019.

WordNet Based Features for Predicting Brain Activity associated with meanings of nouns

Ahmad Babaeian Jelodar, Mehrdad Alizadeh, and Shahram Khadivi
Computer Engineering Department, Amirkabir University of Technology
424 Hafez Avenue, Tehran, Iran

{ahmadb_jelodar, mehr.alizadeh, khadivi}@aut.ac.ir

Abstract

Different studies have been conducted for predicting human brain activity associated with the semantics of nouns. Corpus based approaches have been used for deriving feature vectors of concrete nouns, to model the brain activity associated with that noun. In this paper a computational model is proposed in which, the feature vectors for each concrete noun is computed by the WordNet similarity of that noun with the 25 sensory-motor verbs suggested by psychologists. The feature vectors are used for training a linear model to predict functional MRI images of the brain associated with nouns. The WordNet extracted features are also combined with corpus based semantic features of the nouns. The combined features give better results in predicting human brain activity related to concrete nouns.

1 Introduction

The study of human brain function has received great attention in recent years from the advent of functional Magnetic Resonance Imaging (fMRI). fMRI is a 3D imaging method, that gives the ability to perceive brain activity in human subjects. A three dimensional fMRI image contains approximately 15000 voxels (3D pixels). Since its advent, fMRI has been used to conduct hundreds of studies that identify specific regions of the brain that are activated on average when a human performs a particular cognitive function (e.g., reading, mental imagery). A great body of these publications show that averaging together fMRI data collected over multiple time intervals, while the subject responds to some kind of repeated stimuli (reading words), can present descriptive statistics of brain activity (Mitchell et al., 2004).

Conceptual meanings of different words and pictures trigger different brain activity. The representation of conceptual knowledge in the human brain has been studied by different science communities such as psychologists, neuroscientists, linguists, and computational linguists. Some of these approaches focus on visual features of picture stimuli to analyze fMRI activation associated with viewing the picture (O'Toole et al, 2005) (Hardoon et al., 2007). Recent work (Kay et al., 2008) has shown that it is possible to predict aspects of fMRI activation based on visual features of arbitrary scenes and to use this predicted activation to identify which of a set of candidate scenes an individual is viewing. Studies of neural representations in the brain have mostly focused on just cataloging the patterns of fMRI activity associated with specific categories of words. Mitchell et al present a machine learning approach that is able to predict the fMRI activity for arbitrary words (Mitchell et al., 2008).

In this paper a computational model similar to the computational model in (Mitchell et al., 2008) is proposed for predicting the neural activation of a given stimulus word. Mitchell et al performs prediction of the neural fMRI activation based on a feature vector for each noun. The feature vector is extracted by the co-occurrences of each individual concrete noun with each of the 25 sensory-motor verbs, gathered from a huge google corpus (Brants, 2006). The feature vector of each noun is used to

Proceedings of the NAACL HLT 2010 First Workshop on Computational Neurolinguistics, pages 18–26,
Los Angeles, California, June 2010.

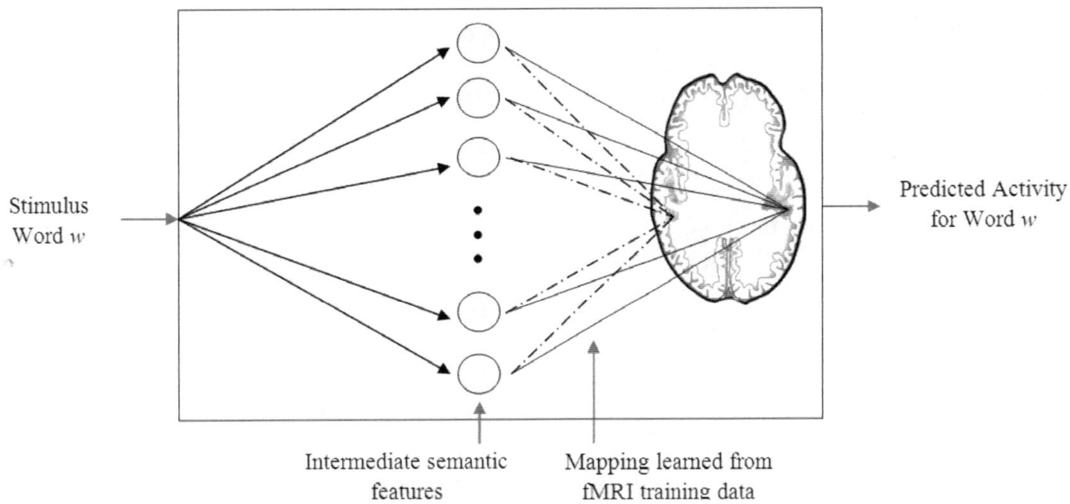

Figure 1 - Structure of the model for predicting fMRI activation for arbitrary stimuli word *w*

predict the activity of each voxel in the brain, by assuming a weighted linear model (Figure 1).

The activity of a voxel is defined as a continuous value that is assigned to it in the functional imaging1 procedure. Mitchell et al applied a linear model based on its high consistency with the widespread use of linear models in fMRI analysis. In this paper focus is on using WordNet based features (in comparison to co-occurrence based features), therefore the linear model proposed and justified by Mitchell et al is used and other models like SVM are not even considered. Mitchell et al, suggests that the trained model is able to predict brain activity even for unseen concepts and therefore notes that a great step forward in modeling brain activity is taken in comparison to the previous cataloging approaches for brain activity. This model does not work well in case of ambiguity in meaning, for example a word like saw has two meanings, as a noun and as a verb, making it difficult to construct the suitable feature vector for this word. We try to alleviate this problem in this paper and achieve better models by combining different models in case of ambiguity.

In our work, we use the sensory-motor verbs which are suggested by psychologists and are also used by (Mitchell et al., 2008), to extract the feature vectors. But, instead of using a corpus to extract the co-occurrences of concrete nouns with these verbs we use WordNet to find the similarities of each noun with the 25 sensory-motor verbs. We also combine the WordNet extracted model with the corpus based model, and achieve better results in matching predicted fMRI images (from the model) to their own observed images.

This paper is organized as follows: in section 2 a brief introduction to WordNet measures is described. In section 3, the WordNet approaches applied in the experiments and the Mitchell et al linear model are explained. The results of the experiments are discussed in section 4 and finally in section 5 the results and experiments are concluded.

2 WordNet-based Similarity

2.1 WordNet

WorNet is a semantic lexicon database for English language and is one of the most important and widely used lexical resources for natural language processing tasks (Fellbaum, 1998), such as word sense disambiguation, information retrieval, automatic text classification, and automatic text summarization.

WordNet is a network of concepts in the form of word nodes organized by semantic relations between words according to meaning. Semantic relation is a relation between concepts, and each node consists of a set of words (*synsets*) representing the

[1] Functional images were acquired on a Siemens (Erlangen, Germany) Allegra 3.0T scanner at the Brain Imaging Research Center of Carnegie Mellon University and the University of Pittsburgh (supporting online material of Mitchell et al. 2008).

real world concept associated with that node. Semantic relations are like pointers between synsets. The synsets in WordNet are divided into four distinct categories, each corresponding to four of the parts of speech – nouns, verbs, adjectives and adverbs (Pathwarden, 2003).

WordNet is a lexical inheritance system. The relation between two nodes show the level of generality in an *is–a* hierarchy of concepts. For example the relation between *horse* and *mammal* shows the inheritance of *horse is-a mammal*.

2.2 Similarity

Many attempts have investigated to approximate human judgment of similarity between objects. Measures of similarity use information found in is–a hierarchy of concepts (or synsets), and quantify how much concept A is like concept B (Pedersen, 2004). Such a measure might show that a *horse* is more like a *cat* than it is like a *window*, due to the fact that *horse* and *cat* share *mammal* as an ancestor in the WordNet noun hierarchy.

Similarity is a fundamental and widely used concept and refers to relatedness between two concepts in WordNet. Many similarity measures have been proposed for WordNet–based measures of semantic similarity, such as information content (Resnik, 1995), JCN (Jiang and Conrath, 1997), LCH (Leacock and Chodorow, 1998), and Lin (Lin, 1998).

These measures have limited the part of speech (POS) of words, for example it is not defined to measure the similarity between verb *see* and noun *eye*. There is another set of similarity measures which work beyond this boundary of POS limitation. These measures are called semantic relatedness measures; such as Lesk (Banerjee and Pedersen, 2003), and Vector (Patwardhan, 2003).

The simple idea behind the LCH method is to compute the shortest path of two concepts in a WordNet unified hierarchy tree. The LCH measure is defined as follows (Leacock and Chodorow, 1998):

$$relatedness_{lch}(c_1,c_2) = -\log\left(\frac{shortestpath(c_1,c_2)}{2D}\right) \quad (1)$$

Similarity is measured between concepts c1 and c2, and D is the maximum depth of taxonomy; therefore the longest path is at most 2D.

Statistical information from large corpora is used to estimate the information content of concepts. Information content of a concept measures the specificity or the generality of that concept.

$$IC(c) = -\log\left(\frac{freq(c)}{freq(root)}\right) \quad (2)$$

freq(c) is defined as the sum of frequencies of all concepts in subtree of concept *c*. The frequency of each concept is counted in a large corpus. Therefore *freq(root)* includes frequency count of all concepts.

The *LCS* (Longest Common Subsummer) of concepts A and B is the most specific concept that is an ancestor of both A and B. Resnik defined the similarity of two concepts as follows (Resnik, 1995):

$$relatedness_{res}(c_1,c_2) = IC(lcs(c_1,c_2)) \quad (3)$$

$IC(lcs(c_1,c_2))$ is the information content of Longest Common Subsummer of concepts *c1* and *c2*.

The Lin measure, augment the information content of the *LCS* with the sum of the information content of concepts *c1* and *c2*. The Lin measure scales the information content of the *LCS* by this sum. The similarity measure proposed by Lin, is defined as follows (Lin, 1998):

$$relatedness_{lin}(c_1,c_2) = \frac{2.IC(lcs(c_1,c_2))}{IC(c_1)+IC(c_2)} \quad (4)$$

$IC(c_1)$ and $IC(c_2)$ are information content of concepts c_1 and c_2, respectively.

Jiang and Conrath proposed another formula named JCN as a similarity measure which is shown below (Jiang and Conrath, 1997):

$$relatedness_{jcn}(c_1,c_2) = \frac{1}{IC(c_1)+IC(c_2)-2.IC(lcs(c_1,c_2))} \quad (5)$$

The Lesk is a measure of semantic relatedness between concepts that is based on the number of shared words (overlaps) in their definitions (*glosses*). This measure extends the glosses of the concepts under consideration to include the

glosses of other concepts to which they are related according to a given concept hierarchy (Banerjee and Pedersen, 2003). This method makes it possible to measure similarity between nouns and verbs.

The Vector measure creates a co–occurrence matrix for each word used in theWordNet glosses from a given corpus, and then represents each gloss/concept with a vector that is the average of these co–occurrence vectors (Patwardhan, 2003).

3 Approaches

As mentioned in the previous section, different WordNet measures can be used to compute the similarities between two concepts. The WordNet similarity measures are used to compute the verb-concept similarities. The feature matrix comprises of the similarities between 25 verbs (features) and 60 concrete nouns (instances). In this section the computational model proposed by (Mitchell et al., 2008), WordNet-based models, and combinatory models are briefly described.

3.1 Mitchell et al Baseline Model

In our paper we used the Mitchell et al regression model for predicting human brain actively as our baseline. In all of the experiments in this paper, we use the fMRI data gathered by Mitchell et al. The fMRI data were collected from nine healthy, college age participants who viewed 60 different word-picture pairs presented six times each (Mitchell et al. 2008). In Mitchell et al, for each concept, a feature vector containing normalized co-occurrences with 25 sensory-motor verbs, gathered from a huge google corpus (Brants, 2006), is constructed. The computational model was evaluated using the collected fMRI data gathered by Mitchell et al. Mean fMRI images were constructed from the primary fMRI images, before training. A linear regression model was trained, using 58 (from 60) average brain images for each subject that maps these features to the corresponding brain image. For testing the model, the two left out brain images were compared with their corresponding predicted images, obtained from the trained model. The Pearson correlation (Equation 6) was used for comparing whether each predicted image has more similarity with its own observed image (*match1*) or the other left out observed image (*match2*).

$$match1(p1=i1\ \&\ p2=i2) = pearsonCorrelation(p1,i1)+ pearsonCorrelation(p2,i2) \qquad (6)$$

p1 ,*p2* are predicted images, and *i1*, *i2* are corresponding observed images.

For calculating the accuracy we check whether the classification is done correctly or not. By selecting two arbitrary concepts (of sixty concepts) as test, there would be 1770 different classifications. The overall percentage of correct classification represents the accuracy of the model.

We tried to use the same implementations in (Mitchell et al., 2008) as our baseline. We implemented the training and test models as described in the supporting online material of Mitchell et al's paper, but due to some probable unseen differences for example in the voxel selection, the classification accuracies achieved by our replicated baseline of Mitchell et al's is in average less than the accuracies attained by (Mitchell et al., 2008). In the test phase we used 500 selected voxels for comparison. The training is done for all 9 participants.

This procedure is used in all the other approaches mentioned in this section. We have contacted the authors of the paper and we are trying to resolve the problem of our baseline.

3.2 WordNet based Models

As mentioned in section 2, several WordNet–based similarity measures have been proposed (Pedersen, 2004). We apply some of the known measures to construct the feature matrix, and use them to train the models of 9 participants.

WordNet::Similarity is a utility program available on web2 to compute information content values. WordNet::Similarity implements measures of similarity and relatedness that are all in some way based on the structure and content of WordNet (Resnik, 2004).

As mentioned in section 2, every concept in WordNet consists of a set of words (synsets). The similarity between two concepts is defined as a series of similarities between synsets of the first concept and synsets of the second concept. In this paper the maximum similarity between synsets of two concepts is considered as the candidate similarity between two concepts.

In contrary to relatedness measures, similarity measures have the limitation of POS of words. In our case the verb-noun pair similarity is not defined when using similarity measures. To solve this problem the sense (POS) of verb features are assumed to be free (verb, noun, adjective and adverb). For most cases the meaning of a verb sense of a word is close to the non-verb senses of that

[2] `http://wn-similarity.sourceforge.net/`

word. For example the verb clean can be seen as a noun, adjective, and adverb which all have close meanings. Some problems arise by this assumption. For example the verb Watch has a far meaning of the noun Watch or some verbs like eat do not have a non-verb sense. To handle these issues the combination of the relatedness measures and similarity measures is used. This approach is discussed in section 3.3 to make a more suitable feature matrix.

The two leave out cross-validation accuracies of regression models trained by feature matrices (computed from WordNet similarities) are depicted in Figure 2. The results helped us to select two measures for a final feature construction. The results are discussed and analyzed in the next section.

3.3 Lin/Lesk and JCN/Lesk based features

The experiments show that, JCN similarity measure gives the best results on extracting the feature vectors for predicting brain activity. Unfortunately, some similarity measures like JCN and Lin feature matrices are to some extent sparse. In some cases, the feature (sensory-motor verb) or even a concept is represented by a null vector. The null input data do not affect the linear regression training, but lead to less data for training the model. This anomaly is originated from the fact that some verbs do not have related non-verb senses (POS).

On the other hand, relatedness measures (like Lesk) do not limit the POS of words. In consequence, we have non-zero values for every element of the feature matrix. This motivates us to combine Lesk similarity measure with Lin to alleviate the defect mentioned above.

Combination is based on finding a better feature matrix from the two Lin (JCN) and Lesk feature matrices. For this, a linear averaging is considered between Lin (JCN) and Lesk feature matrices.

3.4 Combinatory Schemes

In this paper, a new approach for extracting the feature matrix using WordNet is presented and different similarity measures for representing this feature matrix are investigated.

In this section, we propose new combinatory approaches for combining Mitchell et al's corpus based approach with our WordNet based approach. We assume that we have two feature matrices, one based on the corpus-based (baseline) method and the other based on a WordNet-based (Lin/Lesk similarity measure) method.

3.4.1 Linear combination

The first approach for combining WordNet and baseline models, is based on assigning weights $(\lambda, 1-\lambda)$ to the models, for calculation of *match1* and *match2*. *match1* of baseline model is assigned weight λ, and *match1* of WordNet model is assigned weight $(1-\lambda)$, for calculating the final *match1* of the system (Equation 7).

$$match1 = \lambda.(match1Baseline) + (1-\lambda).(match1WordNet) \quad (7)$$

match2 is calculated in the same way. Classification is assumed to be correct when match1 gets a greater value than *match*2. The parameter λ needs to be tuned. Different values of λ were tested and their output accuracies are depicted in Figure 2.

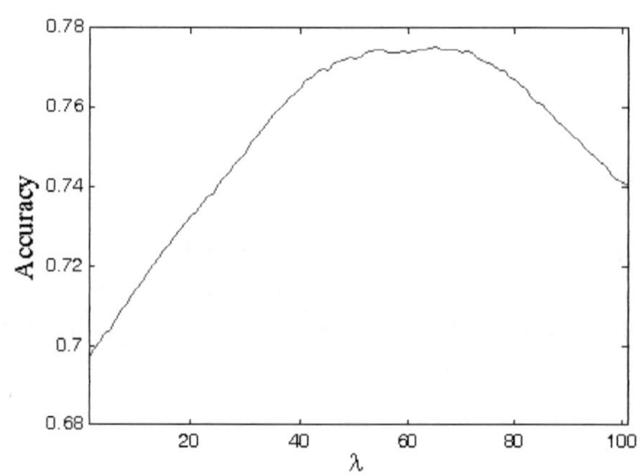

Figure 2 – accuracies of different λ values

3.4.2 Concept based combination

The performance of computational models can be analyzed from a different view. We are looking for a combination mechanism based on model accuracies for classifying a concept pair. This combination mechanism estimates weights for WordNet and baseline models for testing a left out pair. To have a system with the ability to work properly on unseen nouns, we leave out all the concept pairs that have concepts c_1 or c_2 (117 pairs). This guarantees that the trained model is blind to concepts c_1 and c_2. The remaining concept pairs are used for

```
if ( match1Base>match2Base and match1WordNet>match2WordNet
                        or
     match1Base<match2Base and match1WordNet<match2WordNet )
  if ( match1Base-match2Base≥ match1WordNet-match2WordNet
        voteBase++
else if (match1Base>match2Base)
     voteBase++
else
     voteWordNet++
```

Table 1- Voting mechanism

training (1653 pairs).

The accuracies of WordNet and baseline models for the training set are derived and weight of baseline model is calculated as follows:

$$\lambda = \frac{Accuracy(Base)}{Accuracy(Base) + Accuracy(WordNet)} \quad (8)$$

weight of WordNet model is calculated in a similar way. Relation 7 is used for calculating *match1* and *match2*. For calculating the accuracy we check whether the classification is done correctly or not. This procedure is repeated for each arbitrary pair (1770 iterations) to calculate the overall accuracy of the combinatory system.

3.4.3 Voting based combination schemes

In many intelligent combinatory systems, the majority voting scheme is an approach for determining the final output. Mitchell et al collected data for 9 participants. In this approach a voting is performed on the models of 8 participants (*participant j=1:9, j≠i*) for each concept pair (the two left out concepts), to select the better model amongst WordNet and baseline models. The better model is the model that leads to higher accuracy in classifying the left out concepts of 8 participants (*participant j=1:9, j≠i).* The selected model is used to test the model for *pi* (*participant i*).

Votes for selecting the better model for each participant is calculated as shown in Table 1. *match1Base* and *match1WordNet* represent *match1* for baseline and WordNet models.

$$match1 = \frac{voteBase}{8}(match1Base) + \frac{voteWordNet}{8}(match1WordNet) \quad (9)$$

Another approach is linear voting combination. This approach is based on calculating *match1* and *match2* for a model, based on a weighted linear combination (relation 9). The weights for a combinatory model are calculated by a voting mechanism (Table 1).

4 Results and Discussion

As mentioned in section 2, it is possible to construct the feature matrix based on WordNet similarity measures. Seven different measures were tested and models for 9 participants were trained using a 2-leave out cross validation. Four similarity measures (Lin, JCN, LCH, and Resnik), two similarity relatedness measures (Lesk and Vector), a combination of Lin/ Lesk and a combination of JCN/ Lesk are compared to the baseline. The results based on accuracies of these tests are shown in Table 3. The accuracies are calculated from counts of *match scores*. The match score between the two predicted and the two observed fMRI images was determined by which match (*match1* or *match2*) had a higher Pearson correlation, evaluated over 500 voxels with the most stable responses across training presentations.

The results of WordNet-based models are shown in Table 3. As described in section 2 the similarity measures have limitation of POS. The JCN measure has the best accuracy among all single similarity measures. The JCN measure has a better average accuracy (0.65) in comparison to the Lin measure (0.63). The relatedness similarity does not have the limitation of POS. In spite of this advantage the Lesk and Vector measures do not provide a better accuracy than the JCN similarity measure. The Vector average accuracy (0.529) is worse than Lesk (0.622) and therefore just Lesk is considered as a candidate of combination with other similarity measures like JCN and Lin. In section 3 the idea of combining Lin (JCN) and Lesk measures was mentioned. These combinatory schemes led to better accuracies among all single measures (Table 3). Despite the lower average accuracy of the Lin method, the combination of Lin/Lesk achieved a better average accuracy in comparison to JCN/Lesk combination. This is probably because of the lower correlation between Lin/Lesk feature vectors in comparison to JCN/Lesk feature vectors. The correlation between different pairs of feature matrices extracted by WordNet-based similarity measures are shown in Table 2. The result shows that Lesk feature matrix has minimum correlations with all other WordNet-based feature matrices. This is a good motivation to have the Lesk measure as a candidate to mix with other measures to extract a more informative feature matrix. The Lesk feature matrix has the least correlation with Lin feature matrix among all WordNet-based feature matrices. Therefore as noted before, results of Table 3 show better accuracy for Lin/Lesk in comparison to JCN/Lesk. But these accuracies are less than the accuracies attained by the base method proposed by Mitchell et al.

Measure 1	Measure 2	Correlation
Lesk	Lin	**0.3929**
Lesk	Resnik	0.4528
Lesk	JCN	0.5129
Lesk	LCH	0.5556
Lin	LCH	0.6182
JCN	Res	0.6357
JCN	Lin	0.7175
JCN	LCH	0.7234
Lin	Res	0.7400
LCH	Res	0.7946

Table 2– correlation between different pairs of WordNet-based similarity (relatedness) measures

One important reason of this shortage can be the difference in sense (POS) between concepts (with noun POS) and features (with verb POS). This leads to limitation of WorldNet-based measures for constructing better feature matrices. Investigating new features of the same sense of POS between concepts and features (associated with sensory-motor verbs) might lead to even better results.

The Base and WordNet use ultimately different approaches to compute the similarity of each pair of concepts. Several experiments like the union of features and the combination of system outputs was designed. The union of the two feature matrices (baseline feature matrix and Lin/Lesk feature matrix) does not lead to a better result (0.646). In contrary to the united features the combination of these systems gives a better performance. Three different schemes of combinatory systems are proposed in section 4. The first scheme (linear combination) uses a fixed ratio (λ) for combining the output match of the two systems. As depicted in Figure 2 the λ value is tuned and an optimum value of λ=0.64 achieved an average accuracy of 0.775 (Table 4).

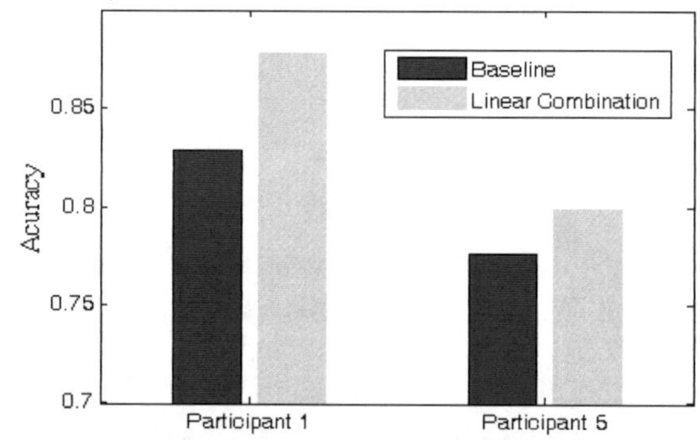

Figure 3- Improvement of linear combinatory scheme

The accuracies of participants *P1* and *P5* for our implemented baseline are almost the same as the accuracies of *P1* and *P5* in Mitchell et al. A comparison of the accuracies for *P1* and *P5* attained by the baseline model and the linear combination scheme is illustrated in Figure 3. The results show considerable improvement in accuracies when the combinatory model is used.

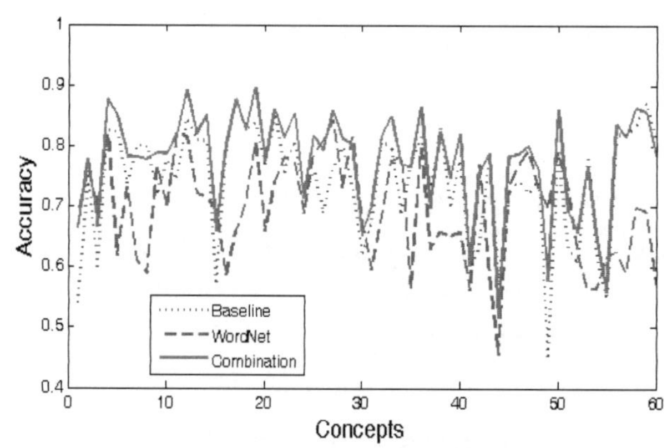

Figure 4- Comparison of linear Combinatory scheme with Baseline and WordNet

Measure/ Participant	P1	P2	P3	P4	P5	P6	P7	P8	P9	Average
Baseline	0.828	0.845	0.752	0.798	0.776	0.658	0.705	0.615	0.680	**0.740**
Lin	0.73	0.624	0.739	0.727	0.591	0.507	0.64	0.501	0.632	0.632
Lesk	0.725	0.629	0.668	0.688	0.601	0.519	0.604	0.584	0.580	0.622
Vector	0.603	0.599	0.551	0.553	0.567	0.451	0.509	0.446	0.476	0.529
LCH	0.685	0.613	0.671	0.617	0.574	0.468	0.577	0.506	0.587	0.589
RES	0.610	0.558	0.594	0.622	0.505	0.555	0.603	0.449	0.490	0.554
JCN	0.797	0.638	0.765	0.713	0.671	0.525	0.504	0.568	0.642	0.647
Lin/Lesk	0.807	0.677	0.767	0.812	0.672	0.645	0.690	0.502	0.697	**0.697**
JCN/Lesk	0.790	0.604	0.718	0.789	0.641	0.593	0.593	0.514	0.667	0.656

Table 3- Results of Different similarity measures compared to baseline

Approach/ Participant	P1	P2	P3	P4	P5	P6	P7	P8	P9	Average
Linear	0.877	0.847	0.827	0.862	0.798	0.696	0.734	0.605	0.728	0.775
Concept-based	0.887	0.832	0.836	0.87	0.793	0.687	0.736	0.588	0.734	0.774
Binary voting	0.894	0.837	0.829	0.858	0.796	0.684	0.758	0.612	0.736	0.778
Weighted voting	0.905	0.840	0.861	0.882	0.808	0.710	0.761	0.614	0.755	0.793

Table 4- Accuracies of different combinatory approaches

The improvement of this combinatory scheme can be viewed from another aspect. Concept accuracy, defined as classification accuracy of the concept paired with each of the other 59 concepts, shows the performance of the system for each concept (Figure 4). The concept accuracies of the linear combinatory scheme are compared with the Baseline and WordNet systems and results are illustrated in Figure 4. The accuracy of some ambiguous concrete nouns like 'saw' are improved in WordNet-based model and this improvement is maintained by linear combinatory model. Improvements have been seen in combinatory model.

The second scheme uses a cross validation of the remaining 58 concepts to train the system, for deciding on each pair of concepts. After training, each system (WordNet and Base) is assigned a weight according to its accuracy. Decision on the test pair is based on a weighted combination of the systems. The results of this scheme are shown in Table 4. It has an improvement of 3.4% in comparison to the baseline model.

The third scheme chooses another combinatory strategy to decide on each test pair of concepts for participant Pi. This scheme gathers votes from the other 8 participants as described in section 3. The results are shown in Table 4. Improvement of binary voting scheme to baseline is almost as much as the Improvement of linear and concept-based schemes to baseline. The weighted voting used a more flexible combination scheme, and led to an improvement of about 5.3% in comparison to baseline.

A result is called statistically significant if it is improbable to have occurred by chance. T-test

Participant	H-value	P-value
P1	1	7.73e-12
P2	0	0.6610
P3	1	5.55e-17
P4	1	2.61e-12
P5	1	0.0051
P6	1	0.0004
P7	1	8.28e-05
P8	0	0.5275
P9	1	3.95e-07

Table 5- t-test of baseline and weighted voting output values for 9 participants

was used to show whether the improvement achieved in this paper is statistically significant or not. The t-test was tested on output accuracies of baseline (with average accuracy 0.74) and weighted voting combinatory scheme (with average accuracy 0.793) for 9 participants. The results are shown in Table 5. The weighted voting scheme does not have improvement on *P2* and *P8* and results are almost similar to baseline, therefore the null hypothesis of equal mean is not rejected (*H-value*=0) at 0.05 confidence level. For all participants with improvement on results, null hypothesis of equal mean is rejected (*H-value*=1) at 0.05 confidence level. This rejection shows that the improvements are approved to be statistically significant for all participants with improvement. The t-test on overall 9 participants rejected null hypothesis with a *P-value* of almost zero. This experiment shows the improvement achieved in this paper is statistical significant.

5 Conclusion

In this work, a new WordNet-based similarity approach for deriving the sensory-motor feature vectors associated with the concrete nouns was introduced. A correlation based combination of WordNet measures is used to attain more informative feature vectors. The computational model trained by these feature vectors are combined with the computational model trained with feature vectors extracted by a corpus based method.

The combinatory scheme achieves a better average accuracy in predicting the brain activity associated with the meaning of concrete nouns. Investigating new features of the same sense (POS) between concepts and non-verb features (associated with sensory-motor verbs) might lead to even better results for WordNet-based Models.

Acknowledgements

The authors would like to thank the anonymous reviewers for their thorough review and their constructive comments.

References

Banerjee, S., and Pedersen, T. 2003. *Extended gloss overlaps as a measure of semantic relatedness*. In Proceedings of the Eighteenth International Joint Conference on Artificial Intelligence, 805–810.

Brants T., and Franz A., 2006, www.ldc.upenn.edu/Catalog/CatalogEntry.jsp?catalogId=LDC2006T13. Linguistic Data Consortium, Philadelphia.

Fellbaum C., 1998. WordNet: *An Electronic Lexical Database*. The MIT Press, Cambridge, MA.

Hardoon D. R., Mourao-Miranda J., M. Brammer, Shawe-Taylor J. 2007. *unsupervised analysis of fMRI data using kernel canonical correlation*. Neuroimage, pp. 1250-1259.

Kay K. N., Naselaris T., Prenger R. J., Gallant J. L. 2008. *Identifying Natural Images from Human Brain Activity*, Nature, pp. 352-355.

Leacock C. and Chodorow M. 1998. *Combining local context andWordNet similarity for word sense identification*. In C. Fellbaum, editor, WordNet: An electronic lexical database, pages 265–283. MIT Press.

Lin D. 1998. *An information-theoretic definition of similarity*. In Proceedings of the International Conference on Machine Learning, Madison.

Mitchell T. M., et al. 2008. *Predicting Human Brain Activity Associated with the Meanings of Nouns*, American Association for the Advancement of Science.

Mitchell T. M., Hutchinson R. A., Niculescu R. S., Pereira F., and Wang X.. 2004. *Learning to Decode Cognitive States from Brain Images*, Machine Learning, pp. 145-175.

O'Toole A. J., Jiang F., Abdi H., and Haxby J. V.. 2005. *Partially distributed representations of objects and faces in ventral temporal cortex*. Journal of Cognitive Neuroscience, pp. 580-590.

Patwardhan S. 2003. *Incorporating dictionary and corpus information into a context vector measure of semantic relatedness*. Master's thesis, University of Minnesota, Duluth.

Pedersen T., Patwardhan S., and Michelizzi J. 2004. *WordNet::Similarity - Measuring the relatedness of Concepts*. Proceedings of Fifth Annual Meeting of the North American Chapter of the Association for Computational Linguistics (NAACL-04), pp. 38-41.

Resnik. P. 1995. *Using information content to evaluate semantic similarity in taxonomy*. In Proceedings of the 14th International Joint Conference on Artificial Intelligence, pages 448–453.

Network Analysis of Korean Word Associations

Jaeyoung Jung
Tokyo Institute of Technology
2-12-1, O-okayama, Meguro-ku
Tokyo, 152-8552, Japan
jung.j.aa@m.titech.ac.jp

Li Na
Tokyo Institute of Technology
2-12-1, O-okayama, Meguro-ku
Tokyo, 152-8552, Japan
li.n.ad@m.titech.ac.jp

Hiroyuki Akama
Tokyo Institute of Technology
2-12-1, O-okayama, Meguro-ku
Tokyo, 152-8552, Japan
akama.h.aa@m.titech.ac.jp

Abstract

Korean Word Associations (KorWA) were collected to build a semantic network for the Korean language. A graphic representation approach of applying coefficients to complex networks allows us to discern the semantic structures within words. A semantic network of the KorWA was found to exhibit the scale-free property in its degree distribution. The growth of the network around hub words was also confirmed through two experimental phases. As an issue for further research, we suggest that the present results may yield insights for computational neurolinguistics, as a semantic network of word association norms can bridge the gap between information about lexical co-occurrences derived from a corpora and anatomical networks as a basis for mapping out neural activations.

1 Introduction

Language is an intricate cognitive system. The mental system, called a grammar by linguists, allows human beings to form and interpret the sounds, words, and sentences of their language. The system is often broken down into several components, such as phonetics, phonology, morphology, syntax, and semantics (O'Grady et al. 2005). Depending on one's concerns, the basic elements of each level (i.e. phones, syllables, morphemes, words, or sentences) become the constituents of linguistic networks of sound patterns, morphological structures, or syntactic organizations. Parse trees, for instance, which are often used in analyzing the syntactic structures of sentences, employ links to represent the *syntagmatic* relationships between words. However, focusing on the processes of conceptualizing feelings, experiences, and perceptions and of encoding them in words (namely, lexicalization), linguists have frequently drawn another kind of linguistic network substantiated as a map of words projecting semantic structures and relations onto an Euclidian space from a *paradigmatic* perspective. In that sense, word association data is attractive in terms of ease of data manipulation, especially when making a graph from a list of word pairs. Moreover, the tools for analyzing complex networks have been often applied to analyzing the structural features within large-scale word association data and to mining lexical knowledge from them.

Since Galton (1880), word association has been used as an empirical method for observing thought processes, memory, and mental states within clinical and cognitive psychology (Deese, 1965). From a linguistic perspective, word associations are undoubtedly valuable language resources because they are rich sources of linguistic knowledge and lexical information. The data has some unique characteristics that are very interesting and useful for cultural studies, reflecting the life styles, social, cultural and linguistic backgrounds of the native speakers who contributed to the data collections. Such information could be particularly useful for further applications not only within semantic studies but also for intelligent information retrieval, brain research, and language learning.

In short, so-called word association norms are crucial as large-scale paradigmatic corpora. They consist of word pair data based on psychological experiments where the participants are typically asked to provide a semantically-related response word that comes to mind upon presentation of a stimulus word. Two well-known word association data for English are the University of South Florida word association, rhyme and word fragment norms

Proceedings of the NAACL HLT 2010 First Workshop on Computational Neurolinguistics, pages 27–35,
Los Angeles, California, June 2010.

(Nelson et al., 1998) and the Edinburgh Word Association Thesaurus of English (EAT; Kiss et al., 1973). For Japanese there are Ishizaki's Associative Concept Dictionary (IACD) (Okamoto and Ishizaki, 2001) and the Japanese Word Association Database (JWAD) (Joyce, 2005, 2006, 2007). Utilizing computational linguistic techniques that aim to mathematically analyze their structures, raw association data is often transformed into some form of graph or complex network representation, where the vertices stand for words and the edges indicate an associative relationship (Miyake et al., 2007). Such techniques of graph representation and their analysis allow us to discern the patterns of connectivity within large-scale resources of linguistic knowledge and to perceive the inherent relationships between words and word groups.

However, despite a long history of word association studies and the valuable contributions of such data to cognitive science, comprehensive, large-scale databases of Korean word association norms have been seriously inadequate. In one study, Lee (1970) surveyed word associations based on 30 adjectives and 29 words representing colors, targeting 40 university students and analyzed the response words for associative tendencies in terms of gender and grammatical word classes. More recently, Shin (1998) attempted to categorize words by conceptual systems in order to construct a lexical dictionary supporting foreign language learners. Although her data differs from word association norms and is not available as an accessible digital database for academic purpose, the semantic classification of the words can be exploited in complementing the analysis of Korean semantic networks.

A collection of Korean word associations (for short, KorWA) was planned and conducted with the strong motivation of constructing a worthwhile database of Korean word associations as a kind of resource that has multiple applications in a number of areas such as lexicography, language education, artificial intelligent, natural language processing, and cultural study. Moreover, we intend to share the database on the web to foster these various potential utilities.

In this paper, KorWA is represented into semantic networks and examined by some combinatorial methods in linguistics. The details are presented from the whole process of collecting the data to the results of the analysis based on the theory of complex networks. Furthermore, this paper briefly discusses another important characteristic, dynamics in scale-free networks, which has recently attracted much attention in this research field. Finally we will mention the applicability of the graph-based analysis developed here to the future potential researches of the computational neurolinguistics.

2 Korean word associations

2.1 Design of Experiment

Preparation of an association experiment begins with the selection of a stimulus word set that is to be presented to the respondent in order to initiate their association process. Determining the stimulus word set is a crucial part in designing the experiment, as associative responses are greatly influenced by the characteristics of the presented words, in particular, the stimulus word familiarity influences response heterogeneity, variability, relational categories, and reaction times (Deese 1965). For the experiment of Korean word associations, we referred to a list of 5,000 Korean basic words (Seo et al. 1998), which was derived from the Yonsei Corpora consisting of 42,644,891 words as of 1998 [ILIS]. From the list, we compiled a list of 3,951 words, consisting of 2,628 nouns, 1,006 verbs, and 317 adjectives.

One hundred and thirty-two native Korean students (71 males and 61 females) at Daejon University, South Korea voluntarily participated in the experiment. The students were mainly from the departments of Korean language and literature (54%), physical therapy (30%), and philosophy (11%). More than 70% of the students had educational background in the humanities. Most of the students (93%) were in their 20s; 82% between 20 and 25 years old and 11% between 26 and 30 years old. 14% of students answered that on average they read more than five books in a month. The task was conducted on the campus of Daejeon University from September 2007 to February 2008. It was a traditional pen-and-paper based task. Under the control of an instructor, each session of the task lasted for 30 minutes.

In the task, participants were instructed to write down the response words that came to mind when they looked at the presented words. We asked the subjects to write down all the words that they could think of from the presented words. This procedure is called the continuous free association task, differing from the discrete association task where the subject is asked to only write down their first response (Cramer 1968).

As a means of naturally displaying continuous associations, the respondents were asked to map out their responses. That is, they drew a kind of associative map for a given word, by adding a line when they made an association and numbering the responses according to the order in which they came to mind from the stimulus word. In the experiment, an A5 size booklet was distributed to the participants. The booklet had 66 pages printed on one-side, including 2 front-back cover pages.

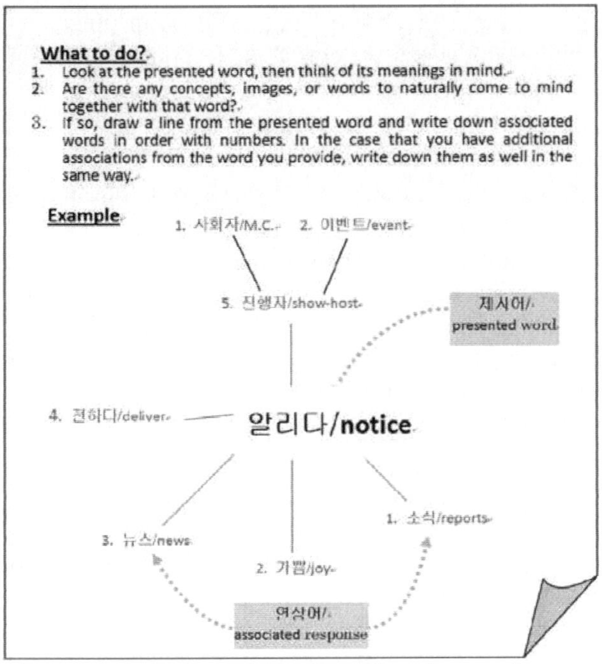

Figure 1. Instructions about the task and example

The first 4 pages contained instructional information; (1) a brief description of the experiment's purpose and its method, (2) a short survey for basic respondent information (gender, age, major, and number of books read in a month), (3) an example illustrating what to do in the task (shown in Figure 1), and (4) one practice before the task. Then, the remaining 60 pages were for the word association task, printed with one word per page. Thus, each participant was asked to provide word association responses for 60 words.

In total, 132 booklets were prepared for the task. A list of 60 words for each booklet was randomly extracted from the 3,951 stimulus set. Apart from six of the 132 sets, the lists included 40 nouns, 15 verbs, and 5 adjectives. The others had slightly different numbers of the syntactic categories. However, eventually each stimulus word was planned to be presented to up to two subjects.

As the result of approximately 6-month period of data collection, we obtained 28,755 responses in total for the 3,942 stimulus words (from the original stimulus set, nine words failed to elicit any word associations). The 28,755 responses (tokens) consisted of 11,275 distinct words (types). Each item was presented to two respondents.

The KorWA database (Figure 2) was constructed from the collected word association responses. The data is arranged into six fields; (1) the part of speech of the stimulus word, (2) the stimulus word, (3) the part of speech of the response, (4) response order, (5) raw form of the response, and (6) response word in standard form.

Stimulus word		Response word			
#1	#2	#3	#4	#5	#6
part of speech	stimulus	part of speech	order	raw form	dictionary form
1	과목	1	1	학교	학교
1	과목	1	1.1	선생님	선생님
1	과목	1	2	수학	수학
1	과목	1	2.1	짜증	짜증
1	젊음	1	1	열정	열정
1	젊음	1	2	도전	도전
1	아버지	1	1	사랑	사랑
1	아버지	1	2	어머니	어머니
1	아버지	1	2.1	사랑	사랑
1	아버지	1	2.2	눈물	눈물
1	열매	1	1	성공	성공
1	열매	1	1.1	열쇠	열쇠
1	열매	1	1.2	노력	노력
1	열매	1	2	사과	사과
1	열매	1	2.1	과일	과일
1	열매	1	2.2	비타민	비타민
1	목적	1	1	지향점	지향점
1	목적	1	1.1	목표	목표
1	목적	2	2	이루다	이루다
...					

Figure 2. Contents of the KorWA database

2.2 Basic Analysis

The Korean word association data collected is briefly summarized here in terms of the relations between the stimulus words and the responses together with some basic statistics. The participants produced on average 218 responses (standard deviation = 63.8, ranging from 98 to 482) for the complete set of 60 words in the free association task, which corresponds to 3.6 responses per stimulus word. Because each stimulus item was presented to two respondents, each stimulus has on average 7.3 association responses.

As already mentioned, our task was the continuous free association task where the respondent was allowed to provide more than one response, so there is the possibility of chaining responses where some association responses are elicited by prior responses. The response set of 28,755 tokens includes all such responses. Furthermore, it is possible to extract the primary responses that were given as the first response produced for each stimulus word. In doing that, it is possible to convert the continuous free association task condition to the discrete association task employed in other existing data. The primary associates for the 3,942 stimulus are 7,550 word tokens (4,197 types). The associations seem to be related to the grammatical classes of the stimulus. Ervin (1961) reports that many associations tend to have the same grammatical class as the stimulus word. Similarly, Jenkins (1954) and Saporta (1955) provide an interesting way of classifying association structures into two modes, i.e. *paradigmatic* associations and *syntagmatic* ones. In the former mode, the stimulus and response fit a common grammatical paradigm. For example, the word ACTION yields the associates of WORDS, LIFE, MOVEMENT, MOTION, GAME, and so on, which are not likely to occur as sequences in everyday English. In the latter case, the stimulus and response are generally contiguous, occupying different positions within phrases or sentences. Namely, they often form sequences, as in the relations between the stimulus word of ADMINISTRATIVE and its common associates of DUTY, JOB, CONTROL, DISCIPLINE, POWER, BUREAUCRATS, POSITION, AGENCY, ENTITY, SCHOOL, BOSS, GOVERNMENT, RULE, etc. (Deese 1965). Deese (1962) clarified the relative frequencies of paradigmatic and syntagmatic associations among the grammatical classes of English, especially with nouns, verbs, adjectives, and adverbs in his study. He observed that the tendency towards paradigmatic or syntagmatic association varied with word class; nouns are dominantly paradigmatic, while adjectives and verbs tend to be both paradigmatic and syntagmatic. In the case of adjectives, it is a particularly interesting tendency for the association types to have a strong correlation with frequency of usage. That is to say, for common adjectives, associations are more likely to be paradigmatic (e.g. for HOT, associates such as COLD, WARM, and COOL more frequently occur than WOMEN, WEATHER, and the like), while uncommon adjectives are more syntagmatic (e.g. for ADMINISTRATIVE, associates such as DUTY, GOVERNMENT, and RULE are more often produced than SUPERVISORY, EXECUTIVE, and so on). What is more, most paradigmatic associates to adjectives are either synonymous with the stimulus (COLD–COOL) or the opposite of the stimulus (COLD–HOT). Common adjectives overwhelmingly have more antonyms as their response, but relatively low-frequent adjectives have more synonym associations.

A similar tendency is observed in our data, which included three types of grammatical class among the stimulus items, with nouns, verbs, and adjectives, covering 66.5%, 25.5%, and 8% of the stimulus set respectively. The different proportions of the word classes reflects their frequencies within the Yonsei corpora, i.e. among the 5,000 most frequent words, there is a much larger number of nouns, compared to verbs and adjectives. By tagging the responses with parts of speech data during the course of constructing the database, we can analyze the distributions of grammatical categories among the responses. The responses were overwhelmingly nouns (78%), followed by adjectives (7%), proper nouns (4.5%) and verbs (4.4%) in descending order. Within the primary response list, the distributions of word class are not greatly different, with 79% nouns, 6.7% adjectives, 4.8% verbs, 3.9% proper nouns, and around 6% others.

Corresponding to the grammatical class of the stimulus specifically, nouns are also the dominant responses. When considering just the primary responses, noun stimulus elicited mostly noun responses (80%), followed by adjectives (6%), proper nouns (5%), and verbs (3%); verb stimulus produced around 80% noun associates, 10% verbs and 4% adjectives; while for adjective stimulus, there were 70% noun responses, 19% adjectives, and 2% verbs. In short, we found a majority of noun–noun, verb–noun, and adjective–noun combinations within the stimulus–response relations. This demonstrates the association tendency for nouns to strongly elicit paradigmatic associations, as seen from the principal noun–noun relations, while verbs and adjectives tend to yield more syntagmatic associations, as seen from the major relations of verb–noun and adjective–noun.

2.3 Network Analysis (1)

Degrees: Recently, a number of studies have applied graph theory approaches in investigating linguistic knowledge resources. For instance, instead of word frequency based computations, Dorow, et al (2005) utilize graph clustering techniques as methods of detecting lexical ambiguity and of acquiring semantic classes. Steyvers and Tenenbaum (2005) conducted a noteworthy study that examined the structural features of three semantic networks (free association norms of Nelson et al., Roget's thesaurus, and WordNet). By calculating a range of statistical features, including the average shortest paths, diameters, clustering coefficients, and degree distributions, they observed interesting similarities between three networks in terms of their *scale-free* patterns of connectivity and *small-world* structures. Following their basic approach, we analyze the characteristics of the semantic network representation of KorWA by calculating the statistical features of the graph coefficients, such as degree and degree distribution.

The semantic network representation of the word association network is constructed by representing the words as nodes and associative pairing information for words as edges. The degree (D) of a node denotes the number of edges that a node has. An undirected graph is structured by the edges, while a directed graph is structured by arcs that include the associative direction. The numbers of incoming and outgoing arcs from a node are referred to as the in-degree and out-degree of a node, respectively. The sum of the in-degree and out-degree values of a node is equal to its total degree.

This concept of graph analysis allows us to categorize the total words in the data into three types; one being words only found in the stimulus set (S-type), one being words occurred as both stimulus and responses (SR-type), and the last being words only observed among the response set (R-type). The proportion of S-type, SR-type, and R-type words in the total word set corresponds to 12.2% (1,568 words), 18.5% (2,374 words), and 69.3% (8,901 words) respectively. Here, it is worth focusing on the SR-type of words. These are words selected as the most frequent ones through a large-scale corpus covering various fields. At the same time, they also are produced by people in the free association task. This may indicate, in some sense, the high usability or commonness of those words. Indeed, the most frequent words in this data all belong to the SR-type.

2.4 Network Analysis (2)

Scale-free: The most frequent words belonging to the SR-type play the role of hubs in semantic networks made from word association data. These hubs can be represented as nodes that have not only outgoing links but also possess ingoing links, which leads us think of a scale-free graph, such as that incorporated within the Barabási-Albert (BA) model. It is widely known that Barabási and Albert (1999) have suggested that the degree distributions of scale-free network structures correspond to a power law, expressed as $P(x=d)=d^{-r}$ (where d stands for degree and γ is a small integer, such as 2 or 3). This type of distribution is also known as Zipf's law, which describes the typical frequency distributions of words in a document and plots on a log scale as a falling diagonal stroke. The degree distribution of nodes in the KorWA network also exhibits this scale-free property, which has also been observed in word association data for different languages.

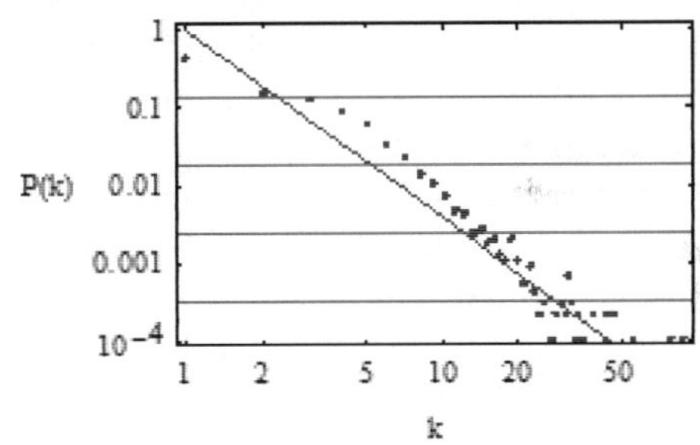

Figure 3. Degree distribution on log-log scales for the KorWA semantic network. P(k) is the probability that a node has k degrees in the network.

However, we should stress the importance of network dynamics and of microscopically examining the ongoing process of data accumulation to determine whether the scale-freeness observed for word association data is derived from the same mechanism as the BA model. Rather than being static, networks are recognized as evolving over time, with the adding or pruning of nodes and edges (Barabási and Albert, 1999; Watts, 1999). Indeed, we can easily identify such networks in a number of areas, from the World Wide Web to the internet connections on a physical level, co-authorships, friendships, and business transactions.

According to the BA model, the probability that a node receives an additional link is proportional to its degree. The probability that a new vertex will be connected to a vertex (node) *i* depends on the connectivity of that vertex. Barabási and Albert (1999) explain with this idea of *preferential attachment* in terms of the scale-free property and the presence of hubs within the network. Networks as dynamical systems which grow over time and have topological properties produce dynamical behaviors as well. In particular with research on the diffusion of a new trend or technology or the spread of a disease and virus, the structural properties of the network have presented a new approach to understanding epidemical behaviors over a network, including issues about why contagion occurs in certain cases, how it spreads, and what is the most efficient and effective way to prevent it. Many researchers have tried to address and analyze such behaviors with small-world models (Ball et al., 1997; Watts and Strogatz, 1998) and scale-free models (Pastor-Satorras and Vespignani, 2001).

The semantic networks that we have examined to date have similar structural properties to many other networks. So, it is also possible to explain the scale-free feature of semantic networks in terms of preferential attachment? How can such dynamic behavior be interpreted for semantic networks? In the next section, we would like to briefly discuss those questions a little further.

2.5 Network Analysis (3)

Network Dynamics: It is a matter of fact that language evolves; especially from a lexical perspective, where new vocabularies are generated and old senses sometimes disappear over time. However, tracing and observing such changes is rather difficult because such natural language evolution occurs over long periods of time. When considering the evolution of semantic networks, therefore, we assume that the growth of a semantic network may correspond to the increases in the numbers of words (nodes) and semantic relations (edges) in as more data is added in the construction of the network. Particularly, for our semantic networks which are built from word association data, the networks grow as more word association data is added.

In this sense, we can attempt to observe the growth process for semantic networks here. To that aim, the KorWA network is particularly suitable, as it is constructed from KorWA data collected from two sessions that used exactly the same task. We may see how the network evolves by taking the sessions as two separate points in time.

From the beginning, the KorWA network starts with the 3,951 nodes that correspond to the set of stimulus words. It cannot be called a network at this stage because there are no links between these nodes. Then, as the word associations are collected, a network starts to appear by adding edges between the initial nodes and new nodes corresponding to the association responses. When the first session of data collection was complete, we found that the initially disconnected 3,951 nodes forming a large, well-connected network, as presented in Table 1.

Table 1. Growth of the KorWA semantic network.

	over time →		
	initially	After 1st session	After 2nd session
Num. of nodes	3,951	9,054	12,844 (Δ 3,790)
Num. of edges	-	13,669	26,931 (Δ 13,262)
Average degree	-	3.02	4.19
Range of degree	-	1 - 87	1 - 198
Num. of components	-	127	14
Num. of nodes in the largest component (%)	-	8,641 (95%)	12,807 (99.7%)
Pseudo diameter of the largest component	-	18	13

The number of nodes had increased to 9,054, and 13,669 edges were generated between them. 8,641 nodes corresponding to 95% of the total nodes are connected to each other, being the largest component in the network, but, at the same time, there were also 126 small partitions with 2 to 3 nodes connected to each. The pseudo diameter, the longest distance, of the largest component is 18, which indicates that the nodes within it are well connected to each other. In this network, a node has three links on average and the distribution of degrees in the network shows a power law distribution ($P(k) \sim K^{-\gamma}$ with a degree exponent $\gamma=2.42$), as in Figure 3 above.

Then, additional word associations were collected for the same set of stimulus words in the same manner as in the first session. When the new data was added to the first network, we obtained a larger network, as described in Table 1. The network grew by 12,844 nodes and 26,931 edges. Through this process, more than 99.7% of nodes (12,807) became interconnected, leaving on 37 words as elements disconnected from the whole graph. Moreover, the pseudo diameter of the largest component became smaller despite the increase in its size. The discrepancy in the degrees of words became larger than before, with a degree range from 1 to 198.

Table 2. Top 20 words with the highest degrees before and after growth of the KorWA network.

Before growth	After growth
돈 ('money')/ 87	공부 ('study')/ 74
사랑 ('love')/ 79	눈물 ('tear')/ 73
친구 ('friend')/ 56	나 ('myself')/ 73
사람 ('human')/ 48	꿈 ('dream')/ 70
물 ('water')/ 48	군대 ('army')/ 69
꿈 ('dream')/45	집 ('house')/ 69
군대 ('army')/ 45	술 ('alcohol')/ 69
마음 ('mind')/ 44	책 ('book')/ 68
집 ('house')/ 43	눈 ('eye/snow')/ 65
눈물 ('tear')/ 43	싸움 ('fight')/64
영화 ('movie')/39	친구 ('friend')/ 64
공부 ('study')/39	영화 ('movie')/ 63
눈 ('eye/snow')/ 36	학교 ('school')/ 63
책 ('book')/ 35	
술 ('alcohol')/ 34	
여자 ('woman')/ 34	
나 ('myself')/ 33	
물건 ('thing')/ 32	
자동차 ('car')/ 32	
가족 ('family')/ 32	

Note. The number after the slash indicates the degree for the word.

Over time (as reflected in the first and second sessions of data collection), 3,790 nodes and 13,262 edges newly appeared in the KorWA network. Through this growth, the network became much more interconnected, as clearly evidenced by the size of the largest component and the pseudo diameter. What is particularly salient is the number of links that a word has through the growth process. Interestingly, regardless of the double increase in the connections within the network, around 60% of the total nodes were still poorly connected, having a degree of only 1 or 2. On the other hand, some of nodes that already had plenty of links became much richer, becoming linked to even more other nodes; with the average degree for 1% of the total nodes being over 60. Table 2 lists the top 20 words in terms of highest degree values before and after growth. The first four words do not change in order, while the shifts for the other top items are not so significant. However, for most of these items, the degree value roughly doubled.

From these observations, we can assume that there are some words that attract more links from other nodes, while most of these other words have just a few connections. This phenomenon appears even more conspicuously through the growth process. The scale-free nature of semantic networks also seems to reflect a kind of preferential attachment. What kinds of words always attract links from new nodes? As suggested already, these seem to be basic concept words, closely related to daily life and culture, and these hubs form a kind of bridge between several different conceptual domains.

Such words contributing to the connectivity of the network are central to the dynamic behavior of across the networks, and are likely to be key concept words for understanding a culture and for learning language within the contexts of semantic networks. Further study and exploration in the structural and dynamic characteristics within semantic networks may open up a new approach to semantics, cultural studies, and language learning from a cognitive perspective.

3 Conclusion and Further study

This paper has described our dataset to represent human language in the form of a network. With much interest in language as a communication and thinking tool, we have sought to build a semantic network representing lexical knowledge and the conceptual relations between words. To that aim, word association data is particularly suitable in terms of its data format and its abundant and useful content. We presented a project to collect Korean word association norms given the high utility and urgent need of data of this kind. We have detailed the project from the design of free association experiment to the basic analysis of the data collected.

The application of the word association data to computational neurolinguistics is an issue for our future work. We believe that our study could potentially represent a breakthrough for this research field. The methods of Mitchell et al. (2008), for example, suggest to us strong connections between neural activation data and lexical co-occurrence information, obtained from text corpora which plays a role of intermediating within linguistics embodiment theory with a sensory-motor basis and amodal theory with computational models. According to Mitchell et al., the techniques of natural language processing combined with neural linguistics can enable us to predict the patterns of neural activation for word stimuli for which fMRI data are not yet available. In short, the neural associations within firing patterns turn out to be correlated with word associations within co-occurrence patterns.

However, the similarity coefficient or the distance between any two words might be computed not only from a set of documents but also from graphic representations of associative concepts, such as the one presented in this paper. If it is true that a word can be represented not only by a three-dimensional array of cerebral activation, but also in terms of the lexical relatedness that is incorporated as a linear combination of these patterns, it may not be an overstatement to say that there might be a structural homology between natural neural networks in the brain and semantic networks built from word association norms. This kind of meta-network perspective within cognitive science has become all the more important because attempts to fill the gaps in the modeling of neural pathways are increasingly attracting wide interest. Sporns et al. (2004), for instance, have tried to apply the conceptual methods of complex networks, such as *small word-scale free*, to cortical networks and to the more dynamic, functional and effective connectivity patterns that underlie human cognition. Similarly, Stam and Reijneveld (2007) have introduced a graph analysis applied to multi-channel recordings of brain activity, by setting up vertices at the anatomical loci within a neural circuit and linking some that elicit high correlation patterns to the same stimulus. Also within the experiment paradigms used by Mitchell et al, some techniques for constructing a network model could be effective for the distributional representation of cortical responses handled at the same level as meaning proximity, even though Mitchell et al. treated each voxel (volumetric pixel value in a 3-dimensional regular grid) independently. If such models of network settings could be applied to images of neural activation across all the voxels for a set of stimulus nouns, it is possible to assume, by a reverse process of parameter estimation, the existence of hidden semantic layers composed of unknown semantic features. These intermediate factors could be compared with real vocabulary data, such as basic verbs (as in the experiment conducted by Mitchell et al.) taking the stimulus nouns as subjects or targets.

Moreover, the merits of introducing graph analysis techniques to computational neurolinguistics could possibly be found in the evolutionary dynamics of networks, to the extent that the degree of word nodes (or, more simply, their frequencies) could be weighted for the neural connectivity deduced from fMRI responses. The data formats of neural activation patterns could then assimilate diachronic data to represent how a network grows over time around the key concepts or hub words, in accordance with the learning processes of particular individuals. Future research from this perspective could also support the high accuracy of similar experiments regardless of distributional bias in word frequencies. Briefly, semantic networks constructed from word association data could convey the lexical co-occurrence of words within documents to a visual map of the human brain reacting to those words.

References

D. Mollison, F. Ball, and G. Scalia-Tomba. 1997. *Epidemics with two levels of mixing*, Annals of Applied Probability 7, pp. 46-89.

A.-L. Barabási, and R. Albert. October 15, 1999. *Emergence of scaling in random networks*. Science, 286:509-512.

P. Cramer. 1968. *Word association*. New York and London: Academic Press.

J. Deese. 1962. "*Form class and the determinants of association*", *Journal of verbal learning and verbal behavior*, vol. 1, pp. 79-84.

B. Dorow, D. Sergi, D. Widdows, E. Moses, K. Ling, and J. Eckmann. 2005. "*Using Curvature and Markov Clustering in Graphs for Lexical Acquisition and Word Sense Discrimination*", in MEANING-2005, 2nd Workshop organized by the MEANING Project.

F. Galton. 1880. "*Psychometric experiments*", *Brain 2*, pp. 149-162.

S. Saporta, 1955. *Linguistic structure as a factor and as a measure in word association*, in J. J. Jenkins (Ed.), *Associative process in verbal behavior*: A Report of Minnesota Conference, Minneapolis: University of Minnesota.

T. Joyce. 2005. *Lexical association network maps for basic Japanese vocabulary*, in Words in Asia cultural contexts, V. B. Y. Ooi, A. Pakir, I. Talib, L. Tan, P. K. W. Tan, and Y. Y. Tan (Eds.). Singapore: National University of Singapore, pp. 114-120.

G. R. Kiss. 1968. *Words associations and networks*, Journal of Verbal Learning and Verbal Behavior, vol.7, pp. 707-13.

Y. J. Lee. 1970. *Comparative studies on word associations by male and female university students: based on adjectives and color-referring words (translated from 남녀 대학생의 언어형상에 관한 비교연구: 형용사와 색채어를 중심으로)*, 아시아 여성 연구 제 9 집. 학술지 344.

C. L. McEvoy and D. L. Nelson. 1982. *Category name and instance norms for 106 categories of various sizes*, American Journal of Psychology 95, pp. 581-634.

H. Akama, J. Jung, M. Miyake, and T. Joyce. 2007. *Hierarchical Structure in Semantic Networks of Japanese Word Associations*, PACLIC21 (Pacific Asia Conference on Language, Information, and Computation-2007), pp.321-328.

A. Carlson, K. Chang, M. Just, R. Mason, S. Shinkareva, T. Mitchell, and V. Malave. 2008. *Predicting human brain activity associated with the meanings of nouns*. Science, 320:1191–1195.

C. L. McEvoy and D. L. Nelson. 2005. *Implicitly activated memories: The missing links of remembering, In Human learning and memory: Advances in theory and application, C. Izawa and N. Ohta (Eds.)*. Mahwah, NJ and London: Lawrence Erlbaum Associates, , pp 177-198.

J. Archibald, J. Rees-Miller, M. Aronoff, and W. O'Grady. 2005. *Contemporary Linguistics*: *An introduction, 5th ed.* Boston & New York: Bedford/St. Martin's.

J. Okamoto and S. Ishizaki. 2001. *"Construction of associative concept dictionary with distance information, and comparison with electronic concept dictionary (translated from 概念間距離の定式化と既存電子辞書との比較)"*, 自然言語処理, vol. 8, pp. 37-54.

A. Vespignani, and R. Pastor-Satorras. 2001. *Epidemic spreading in scale-free networks*, Physical Review Letter. 86. pp. 3200-3203.

H. S. Shin. 1998. *"Korean vocabulary teaching and semantic dictionary (translated from 한국어 어휘교육과 의미사전)"*, 한국어교육 vol. 9, no.2, pp. 85-104.

G. H. Jin, N. J. Nam, and S. G. Seo. 1998. *"Determination of basic vocabulary for Korean language education as a foreign language (translated from 외국어로서의 한국어 교육을 위한 기초 어휘선정)"*, 1st year of annual report (December 14, 1998), Internationalization of Korean language promotion committee, Ministry of Culture, Sports, and Tourism.

C. C. Hilgetag, D. R. Chialvo, M. Kaiser, and O. Sporns. 9 September 2004. *"Organization, development and function of complex brain networks"*, TRENDS in Cognitive Sciences Vol.8 No.

C. J. Stam, J. C. Reijneveld. 2007. *"Graph theoretical analysis of complex networks in the brain"*. Nonlinear Biomedical Physics.

J. B. Tenenbaum and M. Steyvers. 2005. *"The large-scale Structure of Semantic Networks: Statistical Analysis and a Model of Semantic Growth"*, Cognitive Science 29, pp.41-78.

D. J. Watts and S. Strogatz. June 1998. *"Collective dynamics of 'small-world' networks"*. Nature 393, pp.440–442.

Detecting Semantic Category in Simultaneous EEG/MEG Recordings

Brian Murphy
Centre for Mind/Brain Sciences
University of Trento
corso Bettini 31,
38068 Rovereto, Italy
brian.murphy@unitn.it

Massimo Poesio
Centre for Mind/Brain Sciences
University of Trento
corso Bettini 31,
38068 Rovereto, Italy
massimo.poesio@unitn.it

Abstract

Electroencephalography (EEG) and magnetoencephalography (MEG) are closely related neuroimaging technologies that both measure summed electrical activity of synchronous sources of neural activity. However they differ in the portions of the brain to which they are more sensitive, in the frequency bands they can detect, and to the amount of noise to which they are subject. Since semantic representations are thought to be widely distributed in the brain, this preliminary study considered if the broader coverage offered by simultaneous EEG/MEG recordings would increase sensitivity to these cognitive states. The results showed that MEG data allowed stimuli in two semantic categories (mammals and tools) to be distinguished more accurately, despite some experimental settings that were optimised for EEG. The addition of EEG data did not prove informative, indicating that it may be redundant relative to MEG, even when using dimensionality reduction techniques to combat overfitting.

1 Introduction

Electroencephalography (EEG) and magnetoencephalography (MEG) are similar methods for recording activity in the brain. Both detect signals that are produced by the mixing of neural sources, where each source represents macro-scale synchronisation between the firing of individual neurons. The sum of these activities induce voltages at the scalp that are recorded with EEG, and magnetic fields that are detected with MEG. But the signals yielded by each technique are not identical for several reasons. EEG signals are heavily attenuated and filtered (both in time in space) by the passage through skull and tissue. As a result, MEG signals are less noisy, have finer spatial resolution, capture a wider range of frequencies, and so have the potential to be more informative. Further, the signal footprint of MEG and EEG signals on the brain is not the same: EEG sensors are more sensitive to currents that are radial to the scalp and so predominantly detect activity in the at the top of gyri and the bottom of sulci (the top and bottom of folds in the surface of the brain); while MEG is more sensitive to currents that are tangential to the scalp, and so detects more activity in the side walls of sulci. The high spatial resolution of MEG means that it cannot see as deeply into the brain as EEG can. Finally, MEG sensors of different types (in this case magnetometers and planar gradiometers) are sensitive to magnetic fields of different orientations (see Figure 1): planar gradiometers are most sensitive to current generators of a particular orientation directly under the sensor position; magnetometers record generators that are tangential and peripheral to the sensor area.

The distribution of sensor coverage may be important for the decoding of semantic categories in particular. Neuroimaging evidence suggests that semantic representations may be widely distributed in the brain. For example there are well-established differences in neural activity in the fusiform gyrus that correspond to higher level categories (natural vs non-natural kinds; people vs places - see e.g. Chao et al., 2002); there is also evidence that the

Proceedings of the NAACL HLT 2010 First Workshop on Computational Neurolinguistics, pages 36–44,
Los Angeles, California, June 2010.

Figure 1: Schematic from above of selective sensitivity of three co-located MEG sensors

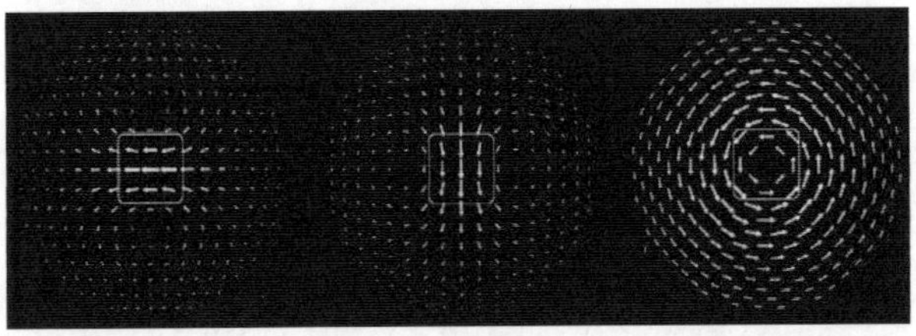

Left and centre panels show perpendicular planar gradiometers; right panel shows magnetometer. A co-located EEG electrode would be most sensitive to currents perpendicular to the scalp. Image courtesy of Elekta AB.

meaning of bodily actions is encoded in the motor-cortex (Pulvermüller, 2005); and concepts associated with eating (e.g. foodstuffs) seem to be represented at least in part by activations in gustatory cortex (Mitchell et al., 2008; Just et al., 2010). Hence a wide coverage of sensors that are sensitive to different but overlapping portions of brain tissue may provide a fuller description of semantic memories.

Given the fact that it has been possible to decode conceptual categories and language semantics from EEG signals (Murphy et al., 2008, 2009), the question is if MEG signals can be shown to be more informative. Similar studies on lower-level tasks typically used in brain-computer interfaces suggests that it may be: Hill et al. (2006) find that there is a modest increase in the decoding accuracy on imagined motor activity with MEG, relative to EEG, and Waldert et al. (2008) have similar findings detecting the direction of hand movements.

A related question is whether the information supplied by EEG and MEG is complementary, and if so how best it should be combined. This depends critically on the number of signals used: raising the number of input signals increases the information supplied to the machine learning methods, but interacts with their tendency to overfit, if the number of descriptive dimensions (recorded signals) is of a similar order of magnitude to the number of training cases (experimental trials in which a stimulus is presented). This is often the case with data from neuroimaging experiments, as there are practical limitations on the number of data points that can be collected: individual stimuli must usually be separated by several seconds so that neural signals can return to baseline between each, and participants can usually only be expected to perform a task at full attention for 60 minutes or so, in such experimental environments.

To investigate this question, we replicated an existing EEG experiment (Murphy et al., 2010). In that experiment participants had been presented with images of animals and tools, while EEG activity was recorded at 64 standard 10-10 locations, and single trials (stimulus presentations) could be classified as representing the category of animal or tool with an average accuracy of 72% over all seven participants. The classification methods used were an adaptive time/frequency window optimisation (Dalponte et al., 2007), a supervised spatial component signal decomposition (Common Spatial Patterns, Koles et al., 1990) that yielded measures of neural activity based on signal power, and a support-vector machine (Boser et al., 1992).

The replication experiment reported here was carried out with two participants, and used the same task and materials, while simultaneously recording with a 306-channel MEG system (204 gradiometers, 102 magnetometers) and a high-density 124-channel EEG system. This data was then analysed using the same machine learning methods as previously, but varying the number and type of input signals, and using dimensionality reduction to address increased dimensionality.

2 Methods

2.1 Experiment and Materials

Two male native speakers of Italian took part in the study, aged 30 and 47. Both were right-handed with corrected or normal vision. Participants in this study receive compensation of 7 euros per hour. The experiment is conducted under the approval of the ethics committee at the University of Trento, and participants gave informed consent.

The participants were asked to perform a silent naming task on grey-scale images of 30 land-mammals and 30 work tools. Each stimulus was presented between four and six times, in randomised order.[1] The participants sat in a relaxed upright posi-

[1] Participant 1 saw 264 stimulus trials (144 mammal and 120 tool trials); participant 2 saw 360 (180 in each class).

tion 1.5m from a projector screen in moderate lighting conditions. Images were presented on a medium grey background and fell within a 6 degree viewing angle. The task duration was split into five blocks and the participants were given the choice to pause between each. The cumulative task time did not exceed 45 minutes.

Each trial began with the presentation of a fixation cross for 0.25s, followed by the stimulus image, a further fixation cross for 0.75s and a blank screen for 1s. Participants were instructed to silently name the object represented in their native tongue (Italian), using the first appropriate label that came to mind, and to press the keyboard space-bar with the left-hand to indicate they had found an appropriate word. If the participant could not think of a suitable label, they were asked not to make a response. The image remained on the screen until the participant responded, or until a time-out of three seconds was reached. The participants were asked to keep still during the task, and to avoid eye-movements and facial muscle activity in particular, except during the blank period.

The materials were chosen to represent well-defined semantic categories and to minimise non-semantic, associative confounds. The set of 30 land mammals were chosen to be both non-domesticated and non-threatening, to avoid emotional valence whether positive (e.g. pets) or negative (e.g. predators). Thirty hardware and garden implements were chosen as genuine work tools. Appropriate photographs were sourced from the internet, and normalised visually: each image file measured 300 pixels square; the image proper was converted to greyscale, superimposed on a homogeneous light-grey background and had maximal horizontal and vertical dimensions of 250 pixels; image contrast was normalised. The concepts represented are listed below.

Land Mammals ant-eater, armadillo, badger, beaver, bison, boar, camel, chamois, chimpanzee, deer, elephant, fox, giraffe, gorilla, hare, hedgehog, hippopotamus, ibex, kangaroo, koala, llama, mole, monkey, mouse, otter, panda, rhinoceros, skunk, squirrel, zebra (*Italian* formichiere, armadillo, tasso, castoro, bisonte, cinghiale, cammello, camoscio, scimpanz, cervo, elefante, volpe, giraffa, gorilla, coniglio, riccio, ippopotamo, stambecco, canguro, koala, lama, talpa, scimmia, topo, lontra, panda, rinoceronte, puzzola, scoiattolo, zebra)

Work Tools Allen key, axe, chainsaw, craft-knife, crowbar, file, garden fork, garden trowel, hacksaw, hammer, mallet, nail, paint brush, paint roller, penknife, pick-axe, plaster trowel, pliers, plunger, pneumatic drill, power-drill, rake, saw, scissors, scraper, screw, screwdriver, sickle, spanner, tape-measure (*Italian* brugola, ascia, motosega, taglierino, piede di porco, lima, forcone, paletta, seghetto, martello, mazza, chiodo, pennello, rullo, coltellino svizzero, piccone, cazzuola, pinza, stura lavandini, martello pneumatico, trapano, rastrello, sega, forbici, spatola, vite, cacciavite, falce, chiave inglese, metro)

2.2 Neural Recordings

The experiment was conducted at the LNiF imaging laboratories at the University of Trento, using a 306-sensor Elekta Neuromag system (2 planar gradiometers and 1 magnetometer at each of 102 sensor locations). A dense-coverage 124-electrode EEG cap was used also, using a right mastoid reference and forehead ground. Both sets of signals were recorded simultaneously at 1000Hz in a magnetically shielded room. At the start of the session the relative positions of the MEG and EEG sensors were determined using a Polyhemus 3-D digitisation system.

Data preprocessing was conducted using the MNE, FieldTrip and EEGLAB packages.[2] The data was band-pass filtered at 1-50Hz to remove slow drifts in the signal and high-frequency noise, and then down-sampled to 125Hz. Eye and muscle artefacts were not removed, but these lie outside the range of frequencies that were considered in the analysis described below.

[2] Martinos Centre for Biomedical Imaging (http://www.nmr.mgh.harvard.edu/martinos/); Donders Institute for Brain, Cognition and Behaviour (http://www.ru.nl/neuroimaging/fieldtrip); and Schwartz Center for Computational Neuroscience (http://sccn.ucsd.edu/eeglab/) respectively.

2.3 Analysis

The analysis method first applies a time/frequency filter to select an information-rich band and interval for the distinction of interest; a supervised decomposition to extract components of whole-scalp synchronous activity that are sensitive to this class distinction (Common Spatial Patterns, or CSP – see Parra et al., 2005; Model and Zibulevsky, 2006; Philiastides et al., 2006 for examples of other applications to cognitive neuroscience); and a general purpose machine learning algorithm (Support-Vector Machine or SVM) that uses the resulting measures of signal power to predict the semantic class of each trial. Individual trial epochs are arbitrarily allocated to one of k interlaced partitions of equal size in a k-fold training/evaluation procedure.

The time/frequency filter applied here was adopted from the earlier experiment, as it had been found to provide optimal separation between trials of the two classes over the participants of that study. Using this common window (4-18Hz, 95-360ms after image onset) allows direct comparison between the informativity of each type of sensor, or combination of sensor types. However this may disadvantage MEG, since it is more sensitive to higher frequency activity ($>$ 50Hz), which at least one study has found to vary systematically with semantic classes (Tanji et al., 2005).

The decomposition method used, CSP (Koles et al., 1990), extracts spatial components of electrophysiological activity (linear combinations of raw signals) that correspond to synchronous neural subassemblies. It is a supervised technique that yields signals whose level of activity (measured as signal power) is modulated by the binary class distinction of interest – that is signals that show high power when processing mammal concepts, and low power when processing tool concepts, or vice-versa. CSP identifies C components (where C is the number of input channels) that are ranked by their sensitivity to the class-separation of interest, in terms of optimal variance for the two populations of signals (i.e., high variance between classes and low variance within classes). In this case we selected the first and the last rows of this matrix (Ramoser et al., 2000) as the components that are most representative for the classes mammals and tools, respectively. This procedure can be interpreted as extracting the event-related spectral activity (i.e. the relative event-related synchronisation) of two synchronous neural structures which have been found to have an optimally differential response to the semantic categories of interest.

The final categorisation step is based on a Support-Vector Machine (SVM) classifier (Boser et al., 1992; Vapnik, 1998). The input for each trial consisted of two measures of neural activity extracted from the category-sensitive signal components: the variance of the waveform, which is proportional to signal power. The features were further normalised by taking the log, and scaling to a range of -1 to +1 across all trials. The SVM implementation used was LIBSVM (Chang and Lin, 2001), and default parameters were used (radial basis function kernel, cost parameter of 1, and a gamma value of the inverse of the number of data-points).[3] Test and training data were kept strictly separate at all stages of analysis.

In the results that follow here, these techniques were first applied as before to replicate the previous experiment, but then also with an additional step of dimensionality reduction to address the over-fitting we expected given the dramatically larger number of input channels (up to 430 if all EEG and MEG channels were used, compared to 64 channels in the previous experiment). The signal recorded in any individual channel will be comprised of a mix of genuine neural activity (both relevant and irrelevant to our classification task), systematic noise sources (e.g. 50Hz electrical line noise, eye-movement artefacts, heart-beat artefacts), and additional random noise. And as EEG and MEG channels record activity from partially overlapping portions of brain tissue, there is considerable redundancy between neighbouring channels. Principle Components Analysis (PCA) is a dimensionality reduction technique that addresses both these issues, grouping redundant activity into the first (strongest)

[3] No optimisation of SVM parameters was attempted, as extensive parameter testing in the earlier experiment did not yield any improvements in classification performance. We believe that this is because CSP is in itself a powerful data-mining technique, that here typically yields two simple clusters of data corresponding to each semantic category. We expect a simple linear classifier would have similar performance on this task.

components, and relegating random noise to the last components. Where PCA was used, it was applied directly before the CSP-based extraction of category-specific sources.

3 Results

In the previous EEG experiment, the classification accuracy averaged 72%, but varied substantially from one participant to the next, ranging from 56% to 80%. First we wanted to establish how representative these two new simultaneous MEG/EEG sessions had been, by replicating the EEG-based analysis. To do this, an arbitrary subset of the 60 EEG channels were selected (taking roughly every second channel among the total of 124), the standard time/frequency filter window was applied, and the resulting data was classified using a 5-fold test-training procedure.[4] The first participant's data was typical of the previous cohort, classifying with accuracy of 70% (in this session, accuracy over 61% is significant at $p < 0.05$, using a one-sided binomial test, $n = 264$, $p = 0.54$), while the second participant's data only achieved 52% accuracy (accuracy over 56% significant at $p < 0.05$, $n = 360$, $p = 0.5$).

To get a first impression of the relative informativity of each signal type, the same procedure was performed with subsets of 60 MEG channels: magnetometers alone yielded markedly higher results (78% and 61% for participants 1 and 2 respectively), while planar gradiometers alone gave marginally lower results (67% and 48% respectively).

Next, to examine the effect of increasing the amount of input data, we performed these analyses using all available channels of each type. In one case (participant 1, magnetometers) there was a drop in 5% points, and another (participant 2, magnetometers) an increase of 3% points, but generally this had little effect on results, indicating that in most cases any increase in available information was offset by overfitting.

These results are summarised in the first two columns of in Tables 1 and 2. The tables also show

Table 1: Classification accuracy, participant 1

Type (available signals)	60 ch.	all ch.	60 cp.
EEG (124)	70%	69%	76%
Magnetometers (102)	78%	73%	78%
Gradiometers (204)	67%	66%	71%
Mag.+Grad. (306)	72%	63%	77%
EEG+Mag. (224)	68%	67%	77%
EEG+Grad. (328)	69%	54%	73%
EEG+Mag.+Grad. (430)	72%	55%	77%

ch: raw channel input; cp: PCA component input

significance: 61% at $p < 0.05$; 65% at $p < 0.001$

Table 2: Classification accuracy, participant 2

Type (available signals)	60 ch.	all ch.	60 cp.
EEG (124)	52%	50%	52%
Magnetometers (102)	61%	64%	68%
Gradiometers (204)	48%	51%	60%
Mag.+Grad. (306)	63%	50%	56%
EEG+Mag. (224)	56%	53%	58%
EEG+Grad. (328)	52%	53%	62%
EEG+Mag.+Grad. (430)	58%	51%	55%

ch: raw channel input; cp: PCA component input

significance: 56% at $p < 0.05$; 59% at $p < 0.001$

the results for all possible combinations of the three signal types, and it is apparent that the effect of overfitting is more pronounced for these larger signal sets. And though the base level of classification accuracy is very different for these two participants, both show a similar pattern with respect to signal type and dimensionality: magnetometers are most informative for these semantic distinctions, and all signal types are vulnerable to overfitting effects.

To combat overfitting, we repeated these analyses with dimensionality reduction. Since PCA is an unsupervised technique, the components were derived and extracted in one step over the whole data set. The first (strongest) 60 components were then taken as input to the same analysis procedure as before (CSP-derived signal power estimates fed to the SVM), to give a global description of whole scalp neural activity, presumably with reduced redundancy and noise. As can be seen in the final columns of Tables 1 and 2, this resulted in optimal classification accuracy in almost all cases, both relative to the full collections of signals, and the 60

[4] In each test/training partition, the labelled training data alone was used to derive two category specific scalp-maps. These scalp-maps were used to extract signal components and resulting signal power measures for all trials. The data was then partitioned again along the same folds for SVM training and prediction.

channel subsets.

A serious limitation of these results however is the arbitrary selection of signal subsets. While much of the information recorded between signals is likely redundant, it could be that the random inclusion or exclusion of one channel or component could dramatically affect accuracy, if that signal was particularly informative, or particularly subject to spurious noise. So to have a more comprehensive view, we conducted an exhaustive parameter search through possible subsets of each combination of signal type, increasing set size in steps of five, and calculating average classification accuracy with a moving window of nine points. The results are illustrated in Figures 2 (using the raw signals as input) and 3 (using PCA components of each signal set), and show the average prediction performance across both experimental participants.

Several things stand out when considering the difference between the classification performance using raw signals directly, and dimensionality reduced sets. In the PCA case, the classification accuracy levels start higher, rise faster, and peak earlier in almost all cases. In absolute terms optimum performance is little changed for magnetometer and EEG signals alone (peaking just above 70% and 60% respectively), while gradiometers seem to benefit somewhat (by about 3% points). But the PCA lines are also smoother, reflecting more stability in classification, and so more independence from particular parameter settings.

Common to both plots is that magnetometers are the most informative type, followed consecutively by gradiometers and EEG channels. In terms of mutual redundancy, the information encoded in EEG channels seems to largely be a subset of that encoded by gradiometers (gradiometer performance is not improved by the addition of EEG channels). The interaction of magnetometer data and these signal types is more complex – magnetometer performance is *reduced* by the addition of either or both EEG and gradiometer channels.

4 Conclusion

This paper reports only two sessions of simultaneous MEG/EEG recording, and there were some clear differences in the results for each participant, so the conclusions must be considered tentative. Nevertheless they suggest that EEG data are to a large extent redundant with respect to MEG signals. MEG magnetometers in particular can lead to substantially higher classification accuracy, with smaller numbers of channels, than EEG alone. In the case of the second participant, prediction with EEG signals did not approach significance, while MEG signals allowed highly significant ($p \ll 0.001$) performance. We believe that this advantage is due to the lack of attenuation and higher spatial resolution inherent in MEG, allowing it to pick out individual neural sources with more precision.

Regardless of the signal types chosen, the high dimensionality of the data posed challenges. Any arbitrary subset of channels may leave informative aspects of brain-activity undetected and this led to fluctuating results; but including large numbers of channels invariably leads to overfitting, and consequent falls in classification accuracy. In light of this, a reduction in dimensions that kept most of the global signal intact (in this case a principle components analysis) proved very effective in preventing overfitting, giving reliably superior performance with lower numbers of channels.

While MEG signals proved more informative, there was not always a dramatic difference in performance (peak performance in participant 1 was similar for MEG or EEG; for participant 2 there was a ca. 15% point difference). However this study used a time interval and frequency band in the signal that had been optimised for EEG, so it may be that considering a wider range of frequencies, higher in the spectrum, could allow MEG to achieve better results. Also, though steps were taken to avoid it, slight movements by the participants relative to the MEG apparatus will have compromised the reliability of its signals (EEG does not suffer from the same problem as electrodes are placed directly on the scalp). This could be addressed in future studies with continuous head tracking and correction.

Finally, several variations could be tried to improve the overall classification performance of the system. The spatial decomposition used (CSP) is particularly prone to overfitting (Parra et al., 2005), and could be replaced with less aggressive techniques like Linear Discriminant Analysis. Principle component analysis is a rather brittle technique

Figure 2: Classification accuracy taking subsets of raw signals from sensors of different types, 9-point smoothed

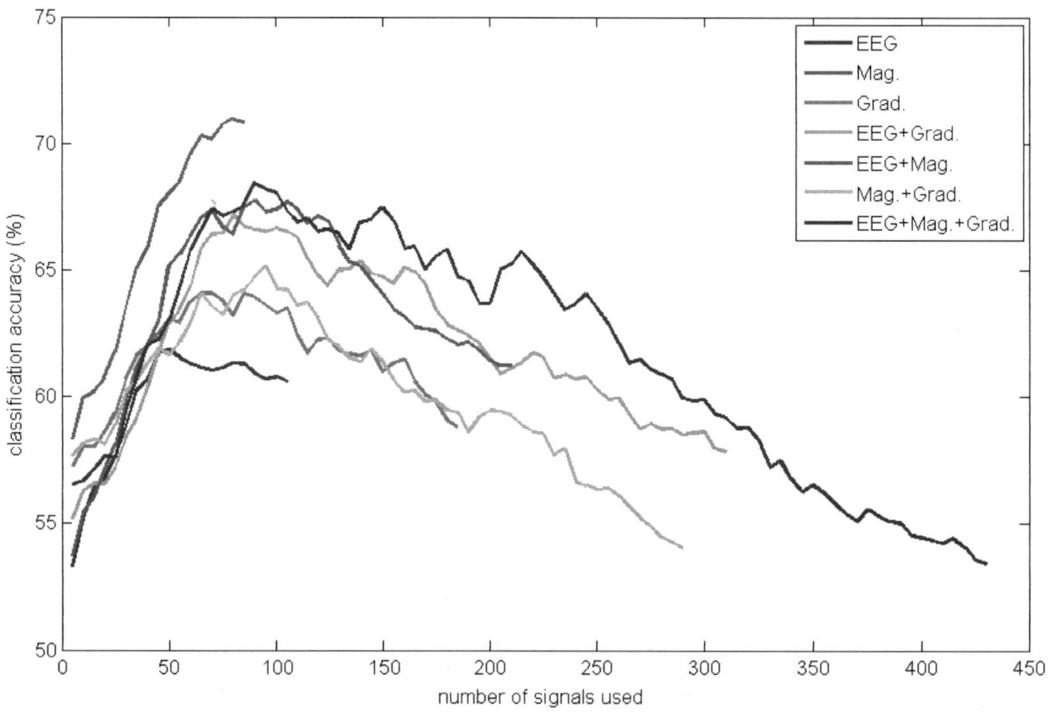

Figure 3: Classification accuracy taking subsets of PCA components derived from raw signals from sensors of different types, 9-point smoothed

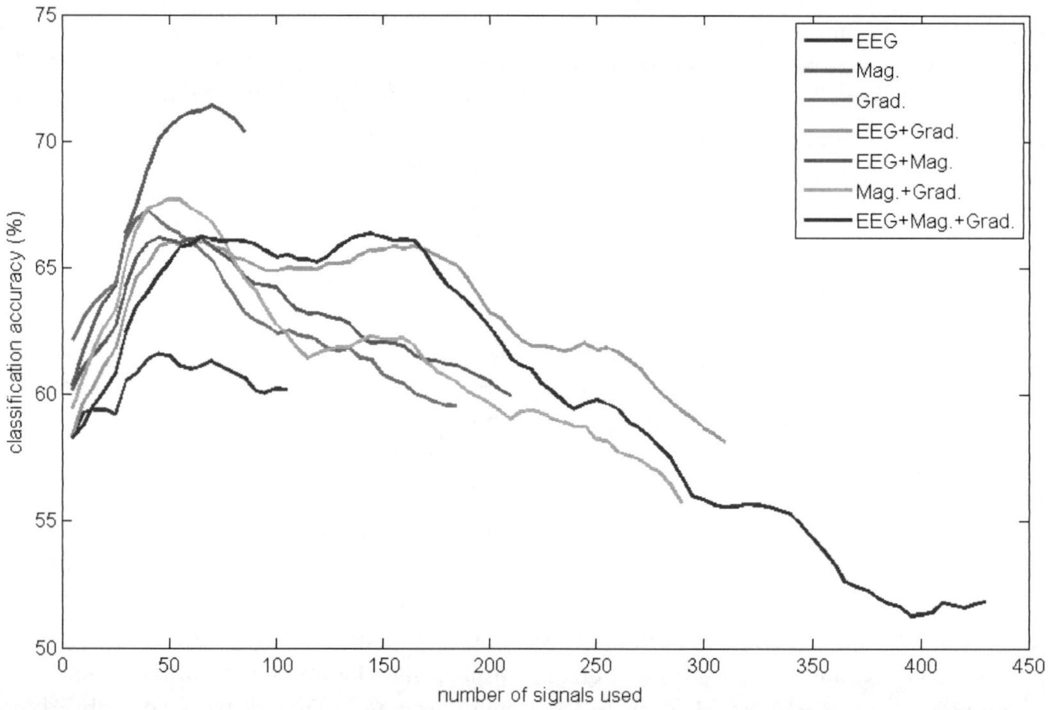

which is heavily biased towards the few strongest sources in a system, and so independent component analysis (ICA) may be a more effective choice for dimensionality reduction (Makeig et al., 1996). And data from the various sensor types could be combined in other ways, using an ensemble of classifiers, each based on different subsets of signals, or by taking more than one class-sensitive component per category.

Acknowledgements

We are very grateful to Elena Betta, Gianpaolo Demarchi and Gianpiero Monittola at the LNiF labs for assistance in MEG data collection. The work described here was funded by CIMeC, the Autonomous Province of Trento, and the Fondazione Cassa Risparmio Trento e Rovereto.

References

Boser, B. E.; I. M. Guyon; and V. N. Vapnik (1992): A training algorithm for optimal margin classifiers. In: *5th Annual ACM Workshop on COLT*, ed. D. Haussler. ACM Press, Pittsburgh, pp. 144–152.

Chang, Chih-Chung and Chih-Jen Lin (2001): *LIBSVM: a library for support vector machines.*

Chao, Linda L.; Jill Weisberg; and Alex Martin (2002): Experience-dependent modulation of category related cortical activity. *Cerebral Cortex*, 12:545–551.

Dalponte, Michele; Francesca Bovolo; and Lorenzo Bruzzone (2007): Automatic selection of frequency and time intervals for classification of EEG signals. *Electronics Letters*, 43:1406–1408.

Hill, N.J.; T.N. Lal; M. Schroder; T. Hinterberger; G. Widman; C.E. Elger; B. Scholkopf; and N. Birbaumer (2006): Classifying event-related desynchronization in EEG, ECoG and MEG signals. *Lecture Notes in Computer Science*, 4174:404.

Just, M.A.; V.L. Cherkassky; S. Aryal; and T.M. Mitchell (2010): A neurosemantic theory of concrete noun representation based on the underlying brain codes. *PLoS ONE*, 5.

Koles, Zoltan J.; Michael S. Lazar; and Steven Z. Zhou (1990): Spatial patterns underlying population differences in the background EEG. *Brain Topography*, 2(4):275–284.

Makeig, Scott; Anthony J. Bell; Tzyy-ping Jung; and Terrence J. Sejnowski (1996): Independent Component Analysis of Electroencephalographic Data. In: *Advances in Neural Information Processing Systems*. MIT Press, vol. 8, pp. 145–151.

Mitchell, Tom M.; Svetlana V. Shinkareva; Andrew Carlson; Kai-Min Chang; Vicente L. Malave; Robert A. Mason; and Marcel Adam Just (2008): Predicting Human Brain Activity Associated with the Meanings of Nouns. *Science*, 320:1191–1195.

Model, Dmitri and Michael Zibulevsky (2006): Learning Subject-Specific Spatial and Temporal Filters for Single-Trial EEG Classification. *NeuroImage*, 32(4):1631–1641.

Murphy, Brian; Marco Baroni; and Massimo Poesio (2009): EEG responds to conceptual stimuli and corpus semantics. In: *Proceedings of the Conference on Empirical Methods in Natural Language Processing*. The Association for Computational Linguistics, pp. 619–627.

Murphy, Brian; Michele Dalponte; Massimo Poesio; and Lorenzo Bruzzone (2008): Distinguishing Concept Categories from Single-Trial Electrophysiological Activity. In: *Proceedings of the Annual Meeting of the Cognitive Science Society*.

Murphy, Brian; Massimo Poesio; Francesca Bovolo; Michele Dalponte; Lorenzo Bruzzone; and Heba Lakany (2010): EEG decoding of semantic category reveals distributed representations for single concepts. *Brain and Language, under review*.

Parra, Lucas C.; Clay D. Spence; Adam D. Gerson; and Paul Sajda (2005): Recipes for the linear analysis of EEG. *NeuroImage*, 28:326–341.

Philiastides, M.G.; R. Ratcliff; and P. Sajda (2006): Neural representation of task difficulty and decision making during perceptual categorization: a timing diagram. *Journal of Neuroscience*, 26(35):8965.

Pulvermüller, Friedemann (2005): Brain mechanisms linking language and action. *Nature Reviews Neuroscience*, 6:576–582.

Ramoser, H.; J. M. Gerking; and Gert Pfurtscheller (2000): Optimal spatial filtering of single trial EEG during imagined hand movement. *IEEE Transactions on Rehabilitation Engineering*, 8(4):441–446.

Tanji, Kazuyo; Kyoko Suzuki; Arnaud Delorme; and Nobukazu Shamoto, Hiroshiand Nakasato (2005): High-Frequency gamma-Band Activity in the Basal Temporal Cortex during Picture-Naming and Lexical-Decision Tasks. *Journal of Neuroscience*, 25(13):3287–3293.

Vapnik, V. N. (1998): *Statistical Learning Theory*. Wiley.

Waldert, S.; H. Preissl; E. Demandt; C. Braun; N. Birbaumer; A. Aertsen; and C. Mehring (2008): Hand movement direction decoded from MEG and EEG. *Journal of Neuroscience*, 28(4):1000.

Hemispheric processing of Chinese polysemy in the disyllabic verb/ noun compounds: an event-related potential study

Chih-ying Huang
Institute of Linguistics
128, Sec. 2, Academia Road, Taipei, Taiwan, R.O.C
evelynhg@alumni.nccu.edu.tw

Chia-ying Lee
Institute of Linguistics
128, Sec. 2, Academia Road, Taipei, Taiwan, R.O.C
chiaying@gate.sinica.edu.tw

Abstract

Through the application of Chinese WordNet, the current study used the manipulation of visual field and the number of senses of the first character in Chinese disyllabic compounds to investigate the representation and the hemispheric processing of related senses in nouns and verbs. In the previous study, Huang et al. (2009) have found the ERP evidence to indicate single entry representation for Chinese polysemy in the left hemisphere; however, in the right hemisphere, they found sense inhibition which may be due to (1) the nature of hemispheric processing in dealing with semantic ambiguity or (2) the semantic activation from the separate-entry representation for senses. To clarify these possibilities, the study used the word class judgment task with the attempt to push subjects in a deeper level of lexical processing. The results revealed sense facilitation effect in the RH and suggested that in a deeper level, the RH had more possibility to observe the sense facilitation due to different efficiency of cerebral hemispheres.

1 Introduction

1.1 Homonymy vs. polysemy

Lexical ambiguity is very common in language. Linguistically, homonymy and polysemy are traditionally distinguished as two types of ambiguity. Early behavioral studies on semantic ambiguity obtained *ambiguity advantage* effects (e.g., Rubenstein et al., 1970; Jastrzembski, 1981, Millis & Button, 1989) in lexical decisions in which ambiguous words yielded faster reaction time than unambiguous words. However, the same results were not replicated in some other studies (e.g., Borowsky & Masson, 1996; Azuma & Van Orden, 1997). More recent psycholinguistic studies found that the so-called ambiguity advantage effects were in fact resulted from the activation of words having related *senses* rather than that of words having unrelated meanings (e.g., Rodd et al., 2002; Beretta et al., 2005; Pylkkänen et al., 2006). These studies were generally in agreement with the linguistic assumption in that homonymy and polysemy might be represented differently in the mental lexicon.

1.2 Hemispheric processing of semantic ambiguity

The issue of hemispheric processing in combination with lexical ambiguity have been widely studied (e.g., Burgess & Simpson, 1988; Beeman & Chiarello, 1998; Faust & Lavidor, 2003) and suggested that both cerebral hemispheres process word meanings in complementary ways. For example, Faust and Lavidor (2003) demonstrated that the LH benefited most from semantically congruent primes related to dominant meaning of ambiguous targets while the RH benefited most from semantically mixed primes. The overall pattern of priming was also suggestive of dissociation in the hemispheric meaning retrieval, with the LH engaging in *fine* semantic coding that focused on a single meaning interpretation, and the RH engaging in *coarser* semantic coding where multiple alternate meanings were activated. Alternatively, Federmei-

Proceedings of the NAACL HLT 2010 First Workshop on Computational Neurolinguistics, pages 45–51,
Los Angeles, California, June 2010.

er and Kutas (1999) offered electrophysiological data in a sentence comprehension task to present another explanation in hemispheric language processing. They suggested that while both hemispheres involved in lexical resolution, they played different roles with the LH being 'predictive', the RH being 'integrative', to complement each other.

Pylkkänen et al., (2006) were the first to focus on the investigation of how different but related senses were psychologically represented in the mental lexicon. Their MEG data suggested the single-entry representation for related senses in the LH whereas they showed the sense inhibition in the RH and interpreted it as a potential sense competition effect. In Chinese, Huang et al. (2009) demonstrated similar patterns in their ERP data in which there was sense facilitation in the LH and sense inhibition in the RH. Nevertheless, the question concerning the representation of related senses in the RH still left unresolved. Early studies on Chinese ambiguity such as Lin (1999) obtained ambiguity advantage but the calculation of 'senses' [1]included related and unrelated meanings and the effect was not reliable enough.

1.3 Ambiguity in Chinese disyllabic compounds

In Chinese words recognition process, the issue of lexical ambiguity involves the composition of constituent characters and how they contribute to the whole word reading. Chinese words differ from English in at least two aspects. First, about 80% of Chinese words are composed of two characters (Huang et al., 2006). Second, unlike the words in English, which every word is composed of letters corresponding to phonemes, Chinese words consist of characters corresponding to morphemes. In other words, each character in Chinese has its morpheme(s) when they are embedded in two-character compounds. Therefore, before we look into the lexical ambiguity of two-character words as lexical items, we should investigate the sense representation of its subcomponent, the representation of its single character within two-character compounds.

In the circumstance which every character in the disyllabic compounds may contribute to word recognition, there still exists disparity between the roles of the first and second character. In light of the studies on the neighborhood size effect, word recognition process will be influenced by the composition of letters or characters. In English, facilitative neighborhood size effects and inhibitory neighborhood size effects were robust findings in low frequency words (e.g. Andrews, 1989, 1992; Grainger and Jacobs, 1996). In the Chinese neighborhood size study (Huang et al., 2006) and eye movement study (Tsai et al., 2006), it was suggested that the neighborhood size of the first character constituent played a more important role in lexical processing than did neighborhood size of the second character constituent. Based on the assumption that the first character will play a key role in whole word reading, the study primarily manipulated the number of senses of the first character and attempted to reveal the hypotheses of sense representation in the context provided by the second character.

The question left in Huang et al. (2009) was that whether the sense inhibition in the RH was due to the nature of hemispheric processing in dealing with semantic ambiguity or the semantic activation from the separate-entry representation for senses. Considering the sense inhibition in the N400 of the ERP component, the pattern in their data was that words having many senses were more negative than those having few senses. That is, there existed competition when the first characters of the targets had many related senses. Nevertheless, based on the single entry assumption for related senses, we assumed sense facilitation for the representation of senses.

In Huang et al. (2009), they required subjects to make word/ non-word lexical decision, but subjects might make their judgments based on perceptual familiarity rather than the involvement of lexical access. Previous studies on probabilistic phonotactics (Vitevitch and Luce, 1998) or on Chinese semantic combinability (Cheng, 2006) have demonstrated opposing effects in early and late levels of word processing. In order to clarify the results in Huang et al. (2009), we designed the

[1] The definition of "sense" in Lin (1999) is different from the "sense advantage effect" demonstrated by Rodd et al. (2002). Lin argued that "meaning" in past research is used as a general term to refer to any kind of linguistic meaning. He claimed that, based upon Ahrens (1999) and Ahrens et al. (1998), it is better to use "sense" and "facets" as a measure index. Though the "number of senses" Lin used is a little different from the "number of meanings" used by Azuma and Van Orden (1997), it is regarded that Lin still did not solve the unreliable findings of ambiguity advantage effect.

word class judgment task to deepen the difficulty of the experimental procedure.

2 The experiment

By changing the depth of the task, the goal of the experiment was to find out if, under the assumption of single entry representation for senses, there was a chance to discover the sense facilitation in the RH. Suppose the representation of Chinese senses had single entry, words having more senses should be less negative than few senses in the N400 because of the benefits of semantic activation. On the contrary, if there were multiple entries for senses in the RH, words of more senses should be more negative than few senses and displayed semantic competition and inhibition.

2.1 Participants

38 college students (18 to28 years of age, mean age 22.39) took part in the experiment (male, right-handedness). Written consent was obtained from all participants. The study was approved by the Taiwan governmental ethics committee.

2.2 Materials

120 Chinese disyllabic compounds, counterbalanced with word class (noun/ verb), were divided into four subsets according to visual field (LVF/ RVF) and NOS of the first character (few/ many senses). Few-sense words were those whose first character senses were from 1 to 3 (mean 1.97) whereas many-sense words were those whose first character senses were over 6 (mean 11.38). Possible confounding factors such as word frequency, NS1, NS2 were controlled.

The number of senses in the current study was collected from the Chinese WordNet, a lexical corpus of Mandarin Chinese and established by Academia Sinica in Taiwan. The corpus attempts to build an up-to-date Chinese lexical network and provides complete information of Chinese word senses.

In Chinese, there exists controversy over the distinction of verbs and nouns. To avoid this problem, the resolutions included: (1) to label the word class according to the system established in Academia Sinica balanced corpus of modern Chinese and (2) to give pilot pretests to another group of people to exclude these possibly confused choices. These subjects were asked to use their language intuition to write down their word-class judgments in a paper sheet containing 120 targets.

Table1. Examples of the stimuli

No. of senses	Word class	RVF	LVF
Few	Noun	笑臉 'a smiling face'	髮夾 'a hair pin'
Few	Verb	猜謎 'to guess a riddle'	服藥 'to take medicine'
Many	Noun	頭獎 'first prize'	綠茶 'green tea'
Many	Verb	彎腰 'to stoop'	掉換 'to ex-change'

2.3 Procedure

Each trial began with a white cross presented centrally for 500 ms. Presentation of the target words appeared on the screen for 150 ms. The disyllabic compound targets were vertically arranged in the left or right visual hemifield with inner edge two degrees of visual angle from fixation. Presentation of numbers from 1 to 9 appeared pseudorandomly in the center of the screen in order to control participants' eyesight. At the end of each trial, a capital B was presented in the center to allow eye blinking for 1500 ms. Participants were asked not to blink their eyes until the appearance to the capital B to minimize the interference of eye movement.

Participants were instructed to judge whether the compound presented was a noun or a verb. For odd-number subjects, they were asked to press the response box with both of their index fingers when the targets were verbs and with both of their middle fingers when the targets were nouns. For even-number subjects, the instruction was the opposite. To control the central fixation of eyes, numbers from 1 to 9 also appeared pseudorandomly. Odd-number subjects should press the response box with both of their index fingers when number 6 to 9 was presented centrally on the screen and with both of their middle fingers when number 1 to 4 was on the screen. For even-number subjects, instruction reversed. Response time and event-related potentials data were both collected during the process.

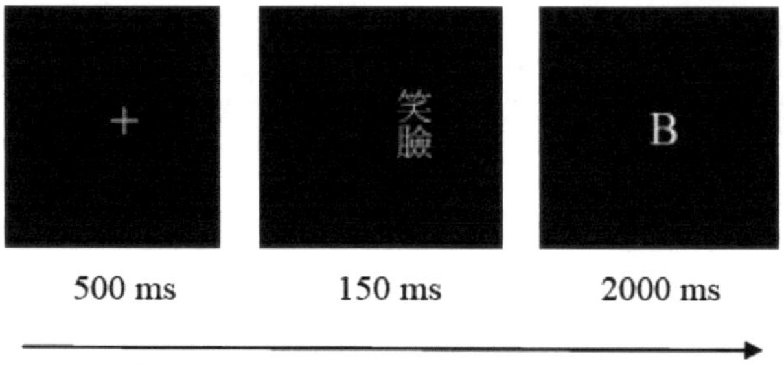

Figure1. Timing diagram of the experimental procedure

2.4 Event-related potential recording

The electroencephalogram was recorded from 64 electrodes embedded in an electro-cap(QuickCap, Neuromedical Supplies, Sterling, Texas, USA), referenced to the left and right mastoid, M1, M2 respectively. Positions of all the electrodes were arranged according to the international ten-twenty system. The electroencephalogram was continuously recorded and digitized at a rate of 500 Hz. The signal was amplified by SYNAMPS2 (Neuroscan Inc., El Paso, Texas, USA) with the band-pass set at 0.5–100 Hz. Blinks and eye movements were monitored via electrodes placed on the infra-orbital ridges of the left eye (VEOG) and the outer canthus left and right electrode (HEOG). A ground electrode was placed on the forehead anterior to the FZ electrode. Electrode impedance was kept below 5 kohms.

2.5 ERP components

In the analyses of the ERP waveforms elicited by every stimulus in each condition, there were typically composed of a negative-going peak at around 100ms (N1), a positive-going peak at around 200ms (P200), a negative-going peak maximizing at around 400 ms (N400) over central and parietal electrode sites. Among these, N 170 was regarded as the early index for visual detection in word processing. In the current study, N170 was used to examine the manipulation of visual field. N400 was characterized as an index sensitive to language-related processing and was generally considered in response to violations of semantic expectations (Kutas and Hillyard, 1980). With the presentation of a semantically inappropriate or incongruent word, a large N400 activity would be elicited. In Huang et al. (2009), the 400 in the RH was regarded as sense competition because words with many senses elicit more negativity at around 400 ms.

3 Results

Behavioral accuracy below 70 percent and ERPs accepted trials below 16 were excluded from ANOVA analyses. Data from 28 of participants were used in the following behavioral and ERP analyses.

3.1 Behavioral data

A 2×2 (number of senses × visual field) analysis of variance (ANOVA) was performed on correct RTs and accuracy. For RTs, no significant main effect of number of senses ($F(1, 27) = 0.5$, $p = .48$) and interaction ($F(1, 27) = 1.33$, $p = .26$) was observed. A main effect of visual field reached marginally significance ($F(1, 27) = 3.38$, $p = .077$). Stimuli presented to RVF/ LH had the tendency to produce shorter response time than those presented to LVF/ RH. For accuracy, not any main effect or interaction was obtained.

3.2 ERP data

Temporal time windows of interest were N170 (150-180 ms) and N400 (350-500 ms). The mean amplitude of each time window from selected electrodes served as dependent measures in a repeated measures analysis of variance (ANOVA).

3.2.1 N170 (150-180 ms)

The mean amplitude of N170 was analyzed by ANOVA with factors of visual field (LVF/RVF), number of senses, and electrodes (P3/P4, P5/P6, P7/P8, PO5/ PO6). We obtained a significant visual field × electrodes interaction $F(7,189) = 45.34$, $p < .001$. Post-hoc comparison indicated that visual field simple main effects reached statistical significance in all electrodes (p's<.001). In electrodes on the left, P3, P5, P7, PO5, right visual field presentation elicited much greater negativity than left visual presentation and vice versa in electrodes on the right, P4, P6, P8, and PO8.

3.2.2 N400 (350-500 ms)

Mean amplitudes of all conditions were measured from 350 to 500ms and subjected to ANOVA with factors of visual field, the number of senses, electrodes, hemispheres. The midline analysis revealed marginal significance of two way interaction between the number of senses and visual field (F (1, 27) =3.83, p=.06). In the lateral analysis, there was marginal significance of visual field by number of senses interaction (F (1, 27) = 3.18, p=.086) and a marginally significant 4-way interaction of visual field, number of senses, electrodes and hemispheres (F (4, 108) =2.53, p=.072). Post-hoc comparisons showed that in the LVF/ RH few senses tended to be more negative than many senses (p<.05) while in the RVF/ LH, few and many senses did not reveal any difference (p=.73).

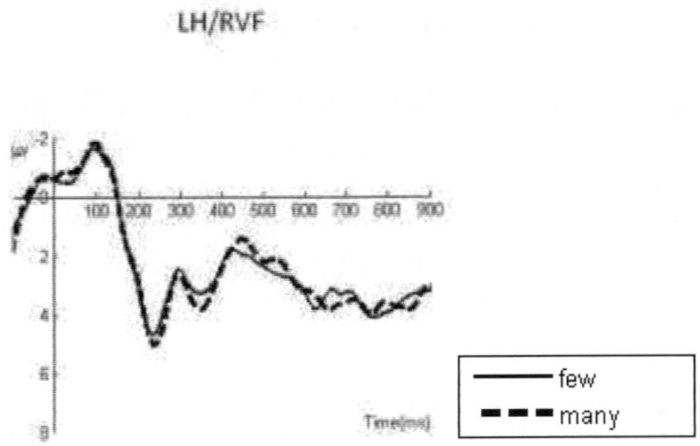

Figure 2—Grand averaged ERPs at CPZ in the RVF/LH.

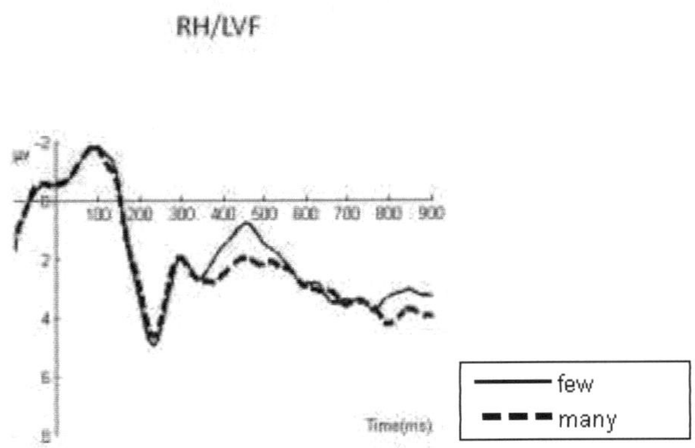

Figure 3—Grand averaged ERPs at CPZ in the LVF/RH

4 Discussion

In the behavioral data, no significant main effect of the number of senses and interaction was observed. Nevertheless, the ERP data demonstrated that there was marginal significance of two-way interaction (visual field x number of senses) and a marginally significant 4-way interaction. Post-hoc comparison showed that there were significant sense facilitation effects in the RH and no effect in the LH. ERP waveforms showed that words of few senses elicited more negativity than words of many senses around 400 ms in the RH, but the two conditions did not differ from each other in the LH.

The marginality of statistical significance led to the speculation in that the word category effect might dilute the sense effect in the experiment. Many studies, in general, suggested that the neural systems for lexical processing of nouns and verbs were anatomically distinct. For example, in children's lexical development, the acquisition of nouns seems to be earlier and easier than that of verbs (Gentner, 1982). In aphasic findings, case studies indicated that patients with lesions located in left anterior and middle temporal lobe, outside so called language areas, had difficulty in the production of nouns whereas patients with lesions areas in left frontal premotor cortex had difficulty in the production of verbs (Damasio & Damasio, 1992; Damasio et al., 1993). Evidence from event-related potentials also disclosed electrocortical differences between nouns and verbs over widespread cortical areas (Pulvermüller et al., 1999). Therefore, verbs were assumed to elicit stronger electrocortical activity around primary frontal, prefrontal areas associated with motor, premotor functions. Nouns, associated with concrete and well-imaginable meanings related to visual modality, were assumed to elicit larger electrocortical activity around visual cortices.

There was also evidence indicating that the conclusions were oversimplified. For example, Tyler et al. (2001, PET) found no significant action differences for nouns and verbs in lexical decision and semantic categorization task. Similarly, in an fMRI Chinese study, Li et al. (2004) pointed out that nouns and verbs were found to activate a wide range of overlapping brain areas and suggested distributed networks for either word class. One recent Chinese study on concreteness also showed similar distribution over the scalp for both nouns and verbs (Tsai et al., 2008).

The study was not meant to resolve the controversy of neural representations for nous and verbs. Instead, from the marginal significance of the data in the experiment, we speculated that the word class effect may influence the results, which led to the failure to reach significance in overall data. Therefore, we reanalyzed the data with the addition word class as one within-subject factor.

4.1 Re-analyses

To further examine the sense effect in nouns and verbs condition, separate analyses of ANOVA were carried out according to different word classes.

4.2 Behavioral data

A 2x2x2 (number of senses × visual field × word class) analysis of variance (ANOVA) was performed on correct RTs and accuracy. For RTs, results showed marginally significant effects for visual field ($F(1, 27) = 3.38$, $p=.077$) and word class ($F(1, 27) = 2.97$, $p=.096$) and for number of senses × word class interaction ($F(1, 27) = 2.94$, $p=.098$). Stimuli presented to the RVF/ LH tended to responded more quickly than to the LVF/ RH. Stimuli of nouns had shorter response time than stimuli of verbs. For accuracy analysis, nouns had significant higher accuracy than verbs (word class ($F(1, 27) =5.41$, $p<.05$).

4.3 ERP data

The grand mean ERPs elicited by few and many senses in RVF/ LH and LVF/ RH were presented in nouns and verbs separately.

4.3.1 Nouns

In the midline, there was a marginally significant number of senses × electrodes interaction ($F(4, 108) = 2.8$, $p<.08$). Lateral analyses indicated that there was a significant visual field × number of senses × electrode interaction ($F(1, 27) = 3.65$, $p<.05$). Planned comparison showed that only when stimuli presented to the LVF/ RH, few senses were more negative in C, CP, P (p's <.05 to <.01).

4.3.2 Verbs

In the midline analysis, there was no significant main effect of senses or interaction. In the lateral analyses, there were significant interactions of visual field × number of senses ($F(1, 27) =4.69$, $p<.05$) and visual field × number of senses × electrodes × hemispheres ($F(4, 108) = 4.23$, $p<.01$). Planned comparisons of four way interaction showed that when presented to LVF/ RH, few senses were more negative in F3, C3, CP3 and FC4 (p's<.05 to <.01) whereas when presented to the RVF/ LH, there was no difference between few and many senses.

5 Discussion

The purpose of additional analyses of sense effects in nouns and verbs was to examine clearer effects of senses without the confounding of the word class factor. The separate analyses for nouns and verbs both showed significant sense effects in the lateral sites. Furthermore, planned comparison of the senses demonstrated disparate distributions for nouns and verbs respectively. To be more specific, the sense effects for nouns were located in central-to-parietal areas of brain, whereas these effects for verbs primarily showed up in frontal, central, central-parietal electrodes on the left. The re-analyses of ERP data showed that the differences of distribution from either word category diluted the sense effect observed in the first analysis; therefore, the data was only marginally significant in the original analyses. Besides, though the current study was not meant to resolve the representations for different word categories, the additional results seemed to support the distinct neural representations for nouns and verbs, since each word class had its distribution for the sense effects. Certainly, further evidence of Chinese word class was required to approve the statement since there was also evidence suggesting distributed network for Chinese lexical processing (e.g. Li et al., 2004).

According to previous studies, different levels of processing in perception of words would lead to opposing results (e.g. Vitevitch and Luce, 1998; Cheng, 2006). Suppose the results were derived from the single entry representation of senses, the sense effect should be observed in the RH in the experiment since the depth of the task was changed. In other words, when subjects were undergoing a deeper level of lexical processing, the relatedness of senses might have been early processed in the LH due to the engagement in fine semantic processing; on the other hand, the sense effect might appear in the RH because its capacity allowed alternate meanings to maintain. Hence, in a deeper level of task, which slowed down the semantic processing, the facilitative sense effect was observed in the RH.

Overall, we suggested that the representation of Chinese senses be single entry and obtained the sense facilitation effects in LVF/ RH in which few senses were more negative than many senses both in nouns and verbs. We assumed that the results also provided empirical evidence indicating that the construction of Chinese WordNet has psychological validity.

6 Conclusions

The study attempted to find out whether the representation of senses in the RH was single-or separate-entry. When the depth of task was changed, the RH advantage for the processing of semantically related senses was observed. The finding was consistent with recent studies on the representation of polysemy (e.g. Beretta et al. 2005; Pylkkänen et al. 2006, Rodd et al., 2002).

Acknowledgments

This work was supported by grants from Taiwan National Science Council (NSC 94-2411-H-001-068, 95-2413-H-010-002-and NSC 96-2628-H-001-058) and the theme project of brain, cognition and behavioral science from Academia Sinica, Taiwan (AS-93-TP-C05). The authors would like to give gratitude to Jie-Li Tsai, Hsu-wen Huang, Chun-Hsien Hsu and Wen-Hsuan Chan, Chiaju Chou who gave technical support, valuable suggestions and comments on the early draft of this paper.

References

Academia Sinica balanced corpus (version 3). (1998). Academia Sinica, Taipei, Taiwan.

Azuma, T. & Van Orden, G. C. (1997). Why SAFE Is Better Than FAST: The Relatedness of a Word's Meanings Affects Lexical Decision Times. *Journal of Memory and Language, 36*(4), 484-504.

Beretta, A., Fiorentino, R., & Poeppel, D. (2005). The effects of homonymy and polysemy on lexical access: an MEG study. *Cognitive Brain Research, 24*(1), 57-65.

Burgess, C., & Simpson, G. B. (1988). Cerebral hemispheric mechanisms in the retrieval of ambiguous word meanings. *Brain Lang, 33*(1), 86-103.

Damasio A. R. & Daniel, T. (1993). *Nouns and verbs are retrieved with differently distributed neural systems.* Paper presented at the Proceedings of the National Academy of Science.

Faust, M., & Lavidor, M. (2003). Semantically convergent and semantically divergent priming in the cerebral hemispheres: lexical decision and semantic judgment. *Cognitive Brain Research, 17*(3), 585-597.

Federmeier, K. D. & Kutas, M. (1999). Right words and left words: electrophysiological evidence for hemispheric differences in meaning processing. *Cognitive Brain Research, 8*(3), 373-392.

Huang, C-Y, Huang, H-W, Tsai, J-L, Huang, C-C & Lee, C-Y (2009, October). *Number of senses effects of Chinese disyllabic compounds in two hemispheres.* Poster presented at the 13th International Conference on the Processing of East Asian Languages, Beijing Normal University, Beijing, China.

Huang, H. W., Lee, C. Y., Tsai, J. L., Lee, C. L., Hung, D. L., & Tzeng, O. J. (2006). Orthographic neighborhood effects in reading Chinese two-character words. *Neuroreport, 17*(10), 1061-1065.

Kutas, M., & Hillyard, S. A. (1980). Reading senseless sentences: brain potentials reflect semantic incongruity. *Science, 207*(4427), 203.

Lyons, J. (1977). *Semantics.* Cambridge, England: Cambridge University Press.

Pulvermuller, F., Lutzenberger, W., & Preissl, H. (1999). Nouns and Verbs in the Intact Brain: Evidence from Event-related Potentials and High-frequency Cortical Responses. *Cerebral Cortex, 9*(5), 497-506.

Pylkkänen, L., Llinás, R., & Murphy, G. L. (2006). The representation of Polysemy: MEG Evidence. *Journal of Cognitive Neuroscience, 18*(1), 97-109.

Rodd, J., Gaskell, G., & Marslen-Wilson, W. (2002). Making Sense of Semantic Ambiguity: Semantic Competition in Lexical Access. *Journal of Memory and Language, 46*(2), 245-266.

Rubenstein, H., Garfield, L., & Millikan, J. A. (1970). Homographic entries in the internal lexicon. *Journal of Verbal Learning and Verbal Behavior, 9*(5), 487–494.

Vitevitch, M. S., & Luce, P. A. (1998). When Words Compete: Levels of Processing in Perception of Spoken Words. *Psychological Science, 9*(4), 325-329.

An Investigation on Polysemy and Lexical Organization of Verbs

Daniel Cerato Germann[1] **Aline Villavicencio**[12] **Maity Siqueira**[3]
[1]Institute of Informatics, Federal University of Rio Grande do Sul (Brazil)
[2]Department of Computer Sciences, Bath University (UK)
[3]Institute of Language Studies, Federal University of Rio Grande do Sul (Brazil)
{dcgermann,avillavicencio}@inf.ufrgs.br, maitysiqueira@hotmail.com

Abstract

This work investigates lexical organization of verbs looking at the influence of some linguistic factors on the process of lexical acquisition and use. Among the factors that may play a role in acquisition, in this paper we investigate the influence of polysemy. We examine data obtained from psycholinguistic action naming tasks performed by children and adults (speakers of Brazilian Portuguese), and analyze some characteristics of the verbs used by each group in terms of similarity of content, using Jaccard's coefficient, and of topology, using graph theory. The experiments suggest that younger children tend to use more polysemic verbs than adults to describe events in the world.

1 Introduction

Lexical acquisition is restrained by perception and comprehension difficulties, which are associated with a number of linguistic and psycholinguistic factors. Among these we can cite age of acquisition (Ellis and Morrison, 1998; Ellis and Ralph, 2000), frequency (Morrison and Ellis, 1995), syntactic (Ferrer-i-Cancho et al., 2004; Goldberg, 1999; Thompson et. al, 2003) and semantic (Breedin et. al, 1998; Barde et al., 2006) characteristics of words. In terms of semantic features, acquisition may be influenced by the polysemy and generality of a word, among others.

In terms of semantic features, acquisition may be influenced by the generality and polysemy of a word, among others. For instance, considering acquisition of verbs in particular, Goldberg (1999) observes that verbs such as *go*, *put* and *give* are among those to be acquired first, for they are more general and frequent, and have lower "semantic weight" (a relative measure of complexity; Breedin et. al, 1998; Barde et al., 2006). These verbs, known as light verbs, not only are acquired first: they are also known to be more easily used by aphasics (Breedin et al., 1998; Thompson, 2003; Thompson et al. 2003; Barde et al. 2006; but see Kim and Thompson, 2004), which suggest their great importance for human cognition. The preference for light verbs may be explained by the more general meanings they tend to present and their more polysemic nature, that is their ability to convey multiple meanings, since the more polysemic the verb is, the more contexts in which it can be used (Kim and Thompson, 2004; Barde et al., 2006). The importance of the number of relationships a word has in the learning environment has been pointed out by Hills et al. (2009), regardless of generality. Several factors may influence acquisition, but in this paper we will focus on polysemy.

Understanding how characteristics like polysemy influence acquisition is essential for the construction of more precise theories. Therefore, the hypothesis we investigate is that more polysemous words have a higher chance of earlier acquisition. For this purpose, we compare data from children and adults from the same linguistic community, native speakers of Brazilian Portuguese, in an action naming task, looking at lexical evolution by using statistical and topological analysis of the data modeled as graphs (following Steyvers and Tenenbaum, 2005, and Gorman and Curran, 2007). This approach innovates in the sense that it directly simulates the influence of a linguistic factor over the process of lexical evolution.

Proceedings of the NAACL HLT 2010 First Workshop on Computational Neurolinguistics, pages 52–60,
Los Angeles, California, June 2010. ©2010 Association for Computational Linguistics

This paper is structured as follows. Section 2 describes relevant work on computational modeling of language acquisition. Section 3 presents the materials and methods employed in the experiments of the present work. Sections 4 and 5 present the results, and section 6 concludes and presents future work.

2 Related Work

In recent years, there has been growing interest in the investigation of language acquisition using computational models. For instance, some work has investigated language properties such as age-of-acquisition effects (Ellis and Ralph, 2000; Li et al., 2004). Others have simulated aspects of the acquisition process (Siskind, 1996; Yu, 2005; Yu, 2006; Xu and Tenenbaum, 2007; Fazly et al, 2008) and lexical growth (Steyvers and Tenenbaum, 2005; Gorman and Curran, 2007).

Some authors employ graph theory metrics to directly analyze word senses (Sinha and Mihalcea, 2007; Navigli and Lapata, 2007). In this paper, word senses are implicitly expressed by graph edges, thus being considered indirectly. Graph theory has also been successfully used in more theoretical fields, like the characterization and comparison of languages (Motter et al., 2002; Ferrer-i-Cancho et al., 2004; Masucci and Rodgers, 2006). For example, the works by Sigman and Cecchi (2002), and Gorman and Curran (2007) use graph measures to extensively analyze WordNet properties. Steyvers and Tenenbaum (2005) use some properties of language networks to propose a model of semantic growth, which is compatible with the effects of learning history variables, such as age of acquisition and frequency, in semantic processing tasks. The approach proposed in this work follows Steyvers and Tenenbaum (2005), and Gorman and Curran (2007) in the sense of iterative modifications of graphs, but differs in method (we use involutions instead of evolutions) and objective: modifications are motivated by the study of polysemy instead of production of a given topological arrangement. It also follows Deyne and Storms (2008), in the sense that it directly relates linguistic factors and graph theory metrics, and Coronges et al. (2007), in the sense that it compares networks of different populations with the given approach.

As to Brazilian Portuguese, in particular, Antiqueira et al. (2007) relate graph theory metrics and text quality measurement, while Soares et al (2005) report on a phonetic study. Tonietto et al. (2008) analyze the influence of pragmatic aspects, such as conventionality of use, over the lexical organization of verbs, and observe that adults tend to prefer more conventional labels than children.

In this context, this study follows Tonietto et al (2008) in using data from a psycholinguistic action naming task. However, the analysis is done in terms of lexical evolution, by using graph and set theory metrics (explained below) to understand the influence of some linguistic characteristics of words, especially polysemy.

3 Materials and Methods

3.1 The Data

This paper investigates the lexical evolution of verbs by using data from an action naming task performed by different age groups: 55 children and 55 young adults. In order to study the evolution of the lexicon in children, children's data are longitudinal; participants of the first data collection (G1) aged between 2;0 and 3;11 (average 3;1), and in the second collection (G2), between 4;1 and 6;6 (average 5;5) as described by Tonietto et al. (2008). The adult group is unrelated to the children, and aged between 17;0 and 34;0 (average 21;8). The longitudinal data enabled the comparison across the lexical evolution of children at age of acquisition (G1), two years later (G2), and the reference group of adults (G3). Participants were shown 17 actions of destruction or division (Tonietto et al, 2008); answers were preprocessed in order to eliminate both invalid answers (like "I don't know") and answers with only 1 occurrence per group. The selection of this particular domain (destruction and division) is due to its cognitive importance: it was found to be one of the four conceptual zones, grouping a great amount of verbs[1] (Tonietto, 2009).

There were a total of 935 answers per group, out of which 785, 911 and 917 were valid answers to G1, G2 and G3, respectively. These made averages of 46.18, 53.59 and 53.94 valid answers per action, respectively. The average numbers of distinct valid answers per action, before merging (explained in section 3.2), were 6.76, 5.53 and 4, respectively.

[1] The others are evasion, excitation, and union.

The answers given by each participant were collected and annotated two polysemy scores, each calculated from a different source:

- Wscore is the polysemy score of a verb according to its number of synsets (synonym sets) in WordNetBR (Dias-da-Silva et al., 2000, Maziero, 2008), the Brazilian Portuguese version of Wordnet (Fellbaum, 1998).
- Hscore is the number of different entries for a verb in the Houaiss dictionary (Houaiss, 2007).

Information about these two scores for each group is shown in Table 1.

	G1	G2	G3
Average type Wscore	10.55	10.64	10.48
Average token Wscore	16.25	14.66	11.13
Average type Hscore	21.59	20.84	16.26
Average token Hscore	26.93	23.02	17.82

Table 1: Score per group and per participant.

We notice that most scores, i.e., type and token Hscores, and token Wscore, decrease as age increases, which is compatible with the hypothesis investigated. However, due to the limited coverage of WordNetBR[2], some verbs had a null value, and this is reflected in type Wscore. This is the case of "*serrar*" (to saw) which appears in both G1 and G2, but not in G3.

A comparative analysis of linguistic production across the different groups is presented in Table 2. There is a significant similarity across the groups, with 12 verbs (out of a total of 44) being common to all of them. In each column, the second graph is compared to the first. In the "G1-G2" column, there are 16 verbs common to both graphs, which represents 64% of the verbs in G2 (with 36% of the verbs in G2 not appearing in G1). As expected, due to the proximity in age, results show a higher similarity between G1 and G2 than between G2 and G3.

	G1-G2	G2-G3	G1-G3	All
Common verbs	16	17	12	12
Verbs only in older group (%)	36	45.16	58.06	-

Table 2: Comparisons between groups[3].

3.2 Simulation Dynamics

Linguistic production of each group was represented in terms of graphs, whose nodes represent the verbs mentioned in the task. Verbs uttered for the same action were assumed to share semantic information, thus being related to each other. The existence of conceptual relationships due to semantic association is in accordance with Nelson et al. (1998), where implicit semantic relations were shown to influence on recall and recognition. Therefore, for each age group, all the verbs uttered for a given action were linked together, forming a (clique) subgraph. The subgraphs for the different actions were then connected in a merging step, through the polysemic words uttered for more than one action.

As the goal of this research is to investigate whether a factor such as polysemy has any influence on language acquisition, we examine the effects of using it to incrementally change the network over time. Strategies for network modification, such as network growth (Albert and Barabási, 2002), have been used to help evaluate the effects of particular factors by iteratively changing the network (e.g., Steyvers and Tenenbaum, 2005; Gorman and Curran, 2007). Network growth incrementally adds nodes to an initial state of the network, by means of some criteria, allowing analysis of its convergence to a final state. The longitudinal data used in this paper provides references to both an initial and a final state. However, due to differences in vocabulary size and content between the groups, network growth would require complete knowledge of the vocabulary of both the source and target groups to precisely decide on the nodes to include and where. Network involution, the strategy adopted, works in the opposite way than network growth. It takes an older group graph as the source and decides on the nodes to iteratively remove, regardless of the younger group graph, and uses the latter only as a reference for compari-

[2] WordNetBR was still under construction when annotation was performed.

[3] Relevant comparisons are for G1-G2 and G2-G3 pairs. Values for G1-G3 are only presented for reference.

son of the structure and content of the resulting graph.

For comparison, graph theory metrics allow us to measure structural similarity, abstracting away from the particular verbs in the graphs. Since graphs represent vocabularies, by these metrics we aim to analyze vocabulary structure, verifying whether it is possible for structures to approximate each other. The graphs were measured in relation to the following:

- number of vertices (n),
- number of edges (M),
- average minimal path length (L),
- density (D),
- average node connectivity (k),
- average clustering coefficient (C/s)[4],
- average number of repetitions (r).

L assesses structure in the sense of positioning: how far the nodes are from one another. D and k express the relation between number of edges and number of nodes in different ways; they are a measure of edge proportion. C/s measures the distribution of edges among the nodes, assessing the structure *per se*. The division by the number of disconnected subgraphs extends the concept to account for partitioning. Finally, r captures the number of different actions for which the same verb was employed.

Although all metrics are useful for analyzing the graphs, a subset of four was selected to be used in the involution process: k, D, L and C/s. With k and D, we measure semantic share, since that is what relations among nodes are supposed to mean (see above). L and C/s are intended to measure vocabulary uniformity, since greater distances and lower clusterization are related to the presence of subcenters of meaning (again, taking relations as effect of semantic share).

In order to compare the contents of each graph as well, we employed a measure of set similarity; in this case, Jaccard's similarity coefficient (Jaccard, 1901). With these measures, we analyze how close vocabularies of each two groups are in respect to their content. Given two sets A and B, the Jaccard's coefficient J can be calculated as follows:

$$J(A, B) = \frac{x}{(x+y+z)},$$

where "x" is the number of elements in both A and B, "y" is the number of elements only in A, and "z" is the number of elements only in B. For this purpose, graphs were taken as verb sets, regardless of their inner relations.

To verify the hypothesis that more polysemic verbs are more likely to be acquired, by node elimination, verbs were ranked in increasing order of polysemy (from less to more polysemic verbs). Therefore, at each step of graph involution, a verb was selected to be removed, and the resulting graph was measured. In case of a tie, verbs with the same polysemy value were randomly selected until all of them have been removed. Results are reported in terms of the averages of 10-fold cross-validation.

4 Results

A topological analysis of the graphs is shown in Table 3. As expected, vocabulary size, represented by n, increases with age, with G1 and G2 being closer in age and size than G2 and G3. A concomitant decrease in the average connectivity (k) of the nodes with age suggests vocabulary specialization. This decrease is even more clearly shown by density (D), since it measures the proportion of edges against the theoretical maximum. As age increases, so does the average minimal path length (L), with less paths through each node, which leads to a more structured and distributed network. Specialization is again represented by a decrease in r, the average number of actions for which each verb was mentioned (the more repeatedly it is mentioned, the less specialized the vocabulary tends to be).

	G1	**G2**	**G3**
n	22	25	31
L	1.46	1.6	1.98
D	0.55	0.42	0.27
M	128	126	126
C/s	0.84	0.78	0.78
k	μ = 11.64, SD = 6.73	μ = 10.08, SD = 4.86	μ = 8.13, SD = 4.76
r	μ = 5.23, SD = 4.41	μ = 3.76, SD = 3.15	μ = 2.19, SD = 1.58

Table 3: Properties of graphs.

[4] We adopt the local clustering coefficient of Watts and Strogatz (1998), but as the graphs may become disconnected during network modification, this value is further divided by the number of subgraphs.

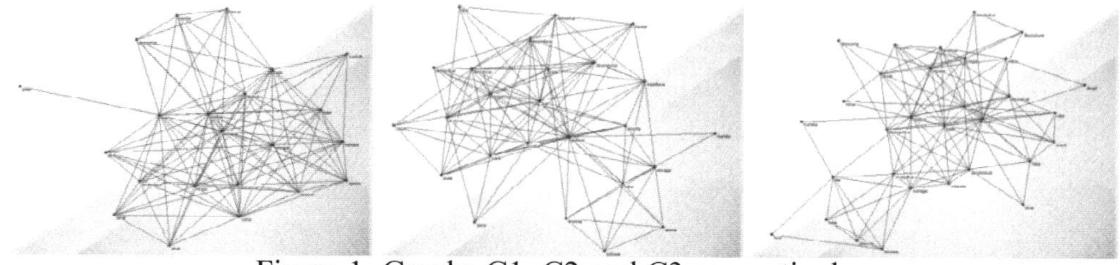

Figure 1. Graphs G1, G2 and G3 respectively.

Results suggest a greater similarity between G1 and G2 than between G2 and G3. Jaccard's coefficient reinforces this result, with a score of 0.52 between G1 and G2, and of 0.44 between G2 and G3.

Figure 1 shows the graphs for each group, where progressive structuring and decentralization can be seen.

The effect of polysemy is observed in the proportion of verbs with a higher degree: G1 is structured by highly connected verbs (there is a low proportion of verbs with low degree), while in G3 more than 80% of the nodes have a degree of 11 or less (Figure 2).

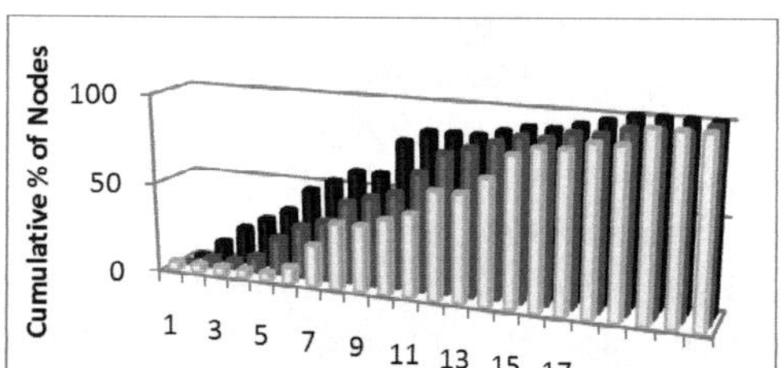

Figure 2. Cumulative histogram of node degree.

5 Simulation Results

This research investigates the relation between the number of meanings and ease of learning, hypothesizing that the more meanings a verb has, the easier it is to be learned, and the earlier children will use it. Particularly considering graph theory metrics, if we remove the verbs with fewer meanings from the graph of an older group, the overall structure will approximate to that of a younger group. Considering set theory metrics, as we remove these verbs, there should be an increase in the similarity between the contents of the graphs.

Therefore, the most relevant part of each chart is its initial state. The verbs to be first removed are expected to be those that differentiate graphs concerning both structure and content.

Although the previous results in section 4 suggest an influence of polysemy on the lexical organization of verbs, we intend to use involutions to confirm these tendencies. Each involution is compared to a random counterpart, making the interpretation easy.

5.1 Network Involution Topology

The graph theory metrics (k, L, C/s and D) of the collected data are shown in Figures 3 and 4 in terms of 2 lines: network involution with node removal (a) by using the selected criterion, and (b) by using random selection (10-fold cross validation). In addition, each figure also shows the measure for the younger group as reference (a dashed, straight, thick line).

In each figure, charts are displayed in four columns and two rows. Each column represents a graph theory metric, and each row refers to the use of a different score. For example, the first chart of each figure is the result of average connectivity (k) in a complete involution, using Wscore. Each legend refers to all eight charts in the figure.

The results of the simulations from G2 to G1 (Figure 3) show that the four metrics are clearly distinct from random elimination from the beginning, indicating that polysemy plays a role in the process. C/s is particularly distinct from random elimination: while the former remains constant almost to the end, indicating a highly structured (clustered) graph, even during node removal, the random elimination shows effects of graph partitioning. The remaining metrics presented their greatest approximations to the reference line before the middle of the chart, suggesting that the initial verbs were actually the ones differentiating both graphs. These results suggest an initial increase in semantic share, as the proportion of edges by node increases (k and D), and in uniformity, as nodes get closer to one another (L) and remain clustered (C/s).

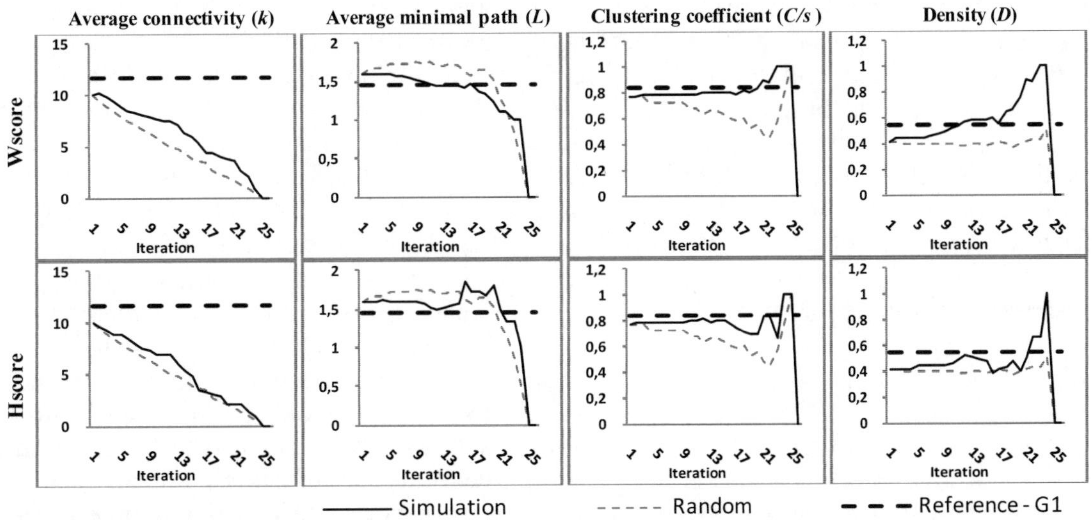

Figure 3. Network involution from G2 to G1 using two scores for node removal: graph theory metrics

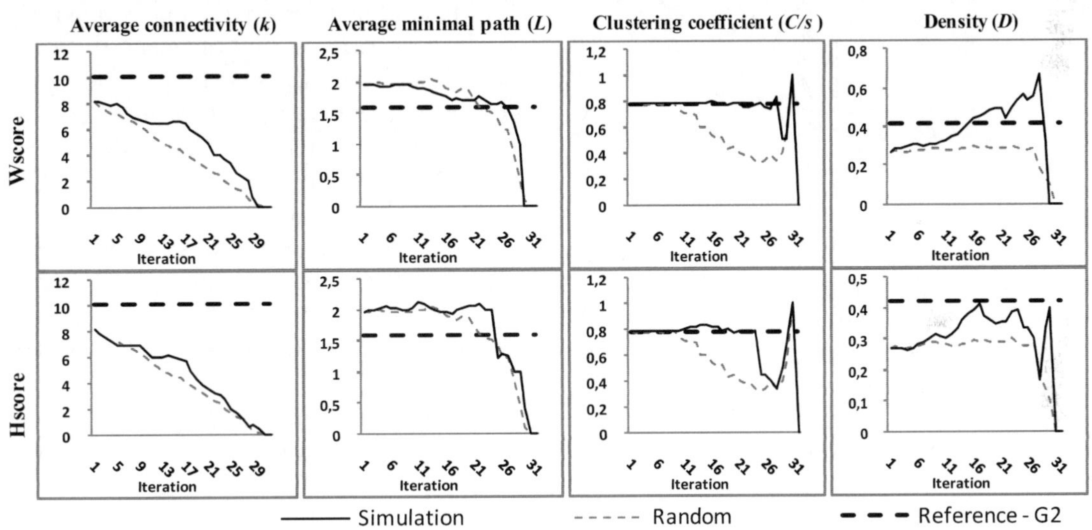

Figure 4. Network involution from G3 to G2 using two scores for node removal: graph theory metrics

Looking at the involution charts of G3, taking G2 as reference, the same tendencies are maintained, although not as clearly as the previous results (Figure 4). The greatest approximations between *k* and *D* happen in the first half of the chart, but much closer to the middle when compared with Figure 3. *C/s* still behaves steadily, remaining stable during most of the simulation, suggesting maintenance of the clustered structure.

The quasi-random behavior of *L* can be explained by the initial structure of the graphs. They become progressively sparser as age increases, but the difference between G3 and G2 is greater than between G2 and G1 (this was both visually and statically confirmed). Therefore, G3 would require too many removals until the most distant nodes were eliminated, even in an ideal elimination simulation, thus preventing a descent from the beginning. The same can be said about average connectivity: since G3 has such a low initial score, and low deviation, even if the nodes with the lowest degrees were eliminated, it would not result in a much better result.

5.2 Network Involution Similarity

The main metric to analyze set similarity is Jaccard's coefficient. There are two important factors influencing it: the number of verbs common to both sets (the "x" component of the formula), "common verbs" hereby; and the number of verbs which are exclusive for the older group, the "different verbs" (the "z" component of the formula, where the older group is represented by "B"). In the charts, a rise means that "different verbs" were eliminated one by one (increasing set similarity), and a descent means that "common verbs" were eliminated instead.

In addition to Jaccard's coefficient, we included the measures for "excluded different" verbs and "excluded common" verbs (and their random counterparts) in percentage. In this sense, the "Excluded Different" line presents the percentage of the "different verbs" excluded so far, and similarly in the "Excluded Common" line. By doing so, it is possible to measure the exact evolution of both sets despite the proportion between them (there are much more "common" than "different" verbs). A rise in the "Excluded Different" line means that sets are getting similar, while stabilization (since descents are not possible) means that they are getting different. The opposite applies to the "Excluded Common" line. All lines start at 0% and end at 100%.

In the figures, charts are arranged in columns (the parameter being measured) and rows (the score being used). This time, each legend is particular to each parameter (one to Jaccard's coefficient and another to the excluded verbs).

Both simulation sets (Figures 5 and 6) confirm the expected pattern: an initial increase in the proportion between "different" and "common" verbs. Jaccard's coefficient behaves more satisfactorily in the second simulation set (Figure 6), where a sharp rise is observed before the middle of the chart, thus indicating that many "different verbs" were excluded. In the first set (Figure 5), Wscore behaves ambiguously with two rises: one before and another after de middle of the chart. Hscore behaves the same way, but the second rise is much sharper than the first. Even so, the positive effect of polysemy is clear in the "Excluded Different" and "Excluded Common" lines. We notice that the "Excluded Different" line is usually above the "Excluded Common" in the beginning and far from the random values. Wscore in Figure 5 is an exception, although a significant rise is observed in the beginning.

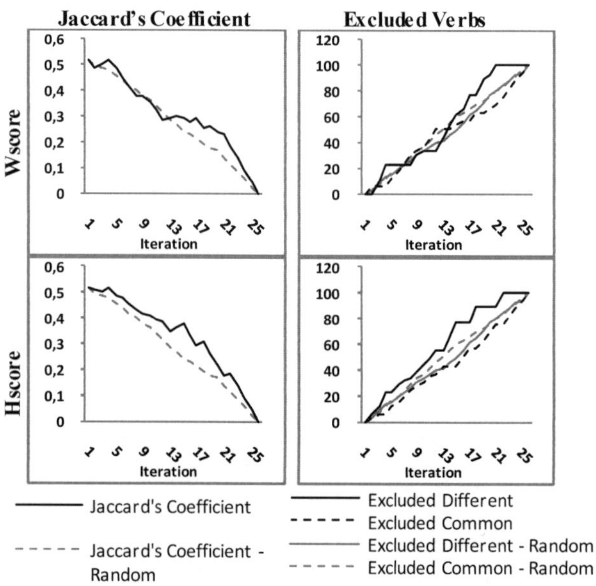

Figure 5. Network involution from G2 to G1 using two scores for node removal: set theory metrics.

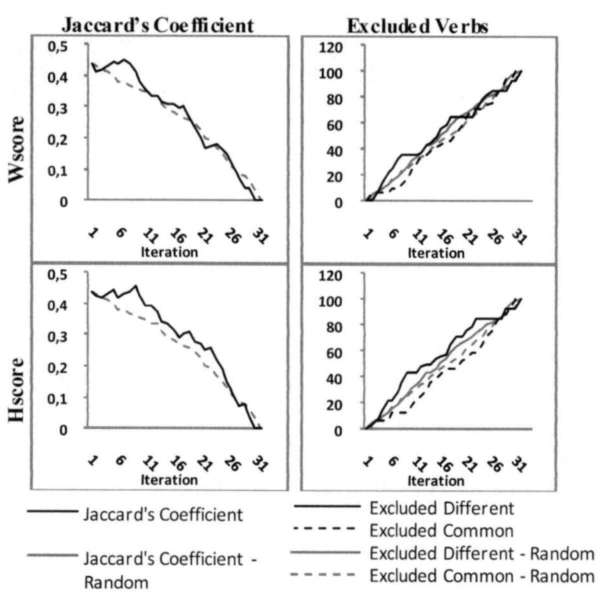

Figure 6. Network involution from G3 to G2 using two scores for node removal: set theory metrics.

5.3 Discussion

Results show that metrics behaved in a consistent manner, considering the natural variation of different sources of information.[5] Concerning graph

[5] Since the measures were taken from the whole graph, it was not possible to determine a measure of significance without other graph configurations to compare to. However, the com-

theory metrics, the early graph disconnection in the random simulation alone (in the *C/s* metric) confirmed a structural stability by using polysemy.

The regular behavior of the Jaccard's coefficient in the simulations may be attributed to a high similarity between the pair of sets: just 45.16% of the verbs in G3 were able to increase the index, and just 36% of the verbs in G2 (Table 2). Even so, an analysis of the "Excluded Different" curves made it clear that the results were better than they appeared to be.

6 Conclusions and Future Work

This study investigated the influence of polysemy on verb acquisition and organization using both graph and set theory metrics. In general, results from the topological analysis showed a tendency towards the reference value, and the greatest similarities were mostly collected in the beginning, as expected, pointing for a preference of children to use more polysemous verbs. The static analysis of the initial graphs (Tables 1, 2 and 3) corroborate the hypothesis. As a result, we note that not only does the evolution of human vocabulary lead to a decrease in the average polysemy measure, but its structure also evolves according to this linguistic factor. So we conclude that both the model of involution and the given analysis are appropriate for linguistic studies concerning vocabulary evolution.

The analyses highlighted also some interesting properties reflected in the graphs, such as vocabulary growth and specialization with the increase of participants' age. In addition, the analysis was useful in showing that the graphs of the two groups of children were more similar to each other than to that of adults, both in structure and content.

For future work, we intend to apply the same approach to other parameters, such as frequency, concreteness, and syntactic complexity. As they may simultaneously influence acquisition, we also plan to investigate possible combinations of these factors. We also intend to apply this methodology to investigate lexical dissolution in the context of pathologies, such as Alzheimer's disease, and in larger data sets, in order to further confirm the results obtained so far.

parisons with random elimination can be seen as a tendency. Additionally, the experiments consist of two simulations, over three different data sets, by using two different sets of polysemy, two kinds of metrics, and five different metrics, which provide robustness to the results.

Acknowledgements

This research was partly supported by CNPq (Projects 479824/2009-6 and 309569/2009-5), FINEP and SEBRAE (COMUNICA project FINEP/SEBRAE 1194/07). We would also like to thank Maria Alice Parente, Lauren Tonietto, Bruno Menegola and Gustavo Valdez for providing the data.

References

Réka Albert and Albert-László Barabási. 2002. Statistical mechanics of complex networks. *Reviews of modern physics*, 74(1):47-97.

L. Antiqueira, M.G.V. Nunes, O. N. Oliveira Jr., and L. da F. Costa. 2007. Strong correlations between text quality and complex networks features. *Physica A: Statistical Mechanics and its Applications*, 373:811-820.

Laura H. F. Barde, Myrna F. Schwartz, and Consuelo B. Boronat. 2006. Semantic weight and verb retrieval in aphasia. *Brain and Language*, 97(3):266-278.

Sarah D. Breedin, Eleanor M. Saffran, and Myrna F. Schwartz. 1998. Semantic Factors in Verb Retrieval: An Effect of Complexity. *Brain and Language*, 63(1):1-31.

Kathryn A. Coronges, Alan W. Stacy, and Thomas W. Valente. 2007. Structural Comparison of Cognitive Associative Networks in Two Populations. *Journal of Applied Social Psychology*, 37(9): 2097-2129.

Simon de Deyne and Gert Storms. 2008. Word associations: Network and semantic properties. *Behavior Research Methods*, 40(1): 213-231.

Bento C. Dias da Silva et al. 2000. Construção de um thesaurus eletrônico para o português do Brasil. In *Proceedings of the 4th Processamento Computacional do Português Escrito e Falado (PROPOR)*, 1-10.

Antônio Houaiss. 2007. *Dicionário Eletrônico Houaiss da Língua Portuguesa*, version 2.0a. Editora Objetiva.

Andrew W. Ellis and Catriona M. Morrison. 1998. Real Age-of-Acquisition Effects in Lexical Retrieval. *Journal of Experimental Psychology: Learning, Memory, and Cognition*, 24(2):515-523

Andrew W. Ellis and Matthew A. L. Ralph. 2000. Age of Acquisition Effects in Adult Lexical Processing Reflect Loss of Plasticity in Maturing Systems: Insights From Connectionist Networks. *Journal of Experimental Psychology: Learning, Memory, and Cognition*, 26(5):1103-1123.

Afsaneh Fazly, Afra Alishahi and Suzanne Stevenson. 2008. A Probabilistic Incremental Model of Word Learning in the Presence of Referential Uncertainty. In *Proceedings of the 30th Annual Conference of the Cognitive Society (CogSci)*.

Christian Fellbaum. 1998. *WordNet: An Electronic Lexical Database*. MIT Press.

Ramon Ferrer i Cancho, Ricard V. Solé, and Reinhard Köhler. 2004. Patterns in syntactic dependency networks. *Phys. Rev. E*, 69(5).

Adele E. Goldberg. The Emergence of the Semantics of Argument Structure Constructions. 1999. In *Emergence of Language*. Lawrence Erlbaum Associates , Mahwah, NJ.

James Gorman and James R. Curran. 2007. The Topology of Synonymy and Homonymy Networks. In *Proceedings Workshop on Cognitive Aspects of Computational Language Acquisition*.

Thomas T. Hills, Mounir Maouene, Josita Maouene, Adam Sheya, and Linda Smith. 2009. *Longitudinal Analysis of Early Semantic Networks: Preferential Attachment or Preferential Acquisition*, 20(6): 729-739.

Paul Jaccard. 1901. Distribution de la flore alpine dans le Bassin des Drouces et dans quelques regions voisines. *Bulletin de la Société Vaudoise des Sciences Naturelles,* 37(140): 241–272.

Mikyong Kim and Cynthia K, Thompson. 2004.Verb deficits in Alzheimer's disease and agrammatism: Implications for lexical organization. *Brain and Language*, 88(1): 1-20.

Ping Li, Igor Farkas, and Brian MacWhinney. 2004. Early lexical development in a self-organizing neural network. *Neural Networks*, 17(8-9): 1345-1362.

A. P. Masucci and G. J. Rodgers. 2006. Network properties of written human language. *Physical Review E*, 74(2).

Erick Galani Maziero, E.G. et al. 2008. A Base de Dados Lexical e a Interface Web do TeP 2.0 - Thesaurus Eletrônico para o Português do Brasil. In P*roceedings of the 6th Workshop em Tecnologia da Informação e da Linguagem Humana*.

Catriona M. Morrison and Andrew W. Ellis. 1995. Roles of Word Frequency and Age of Acquisition in Word Naming and Lexical Decision. *Journal of Experimental Psychology: Learning, Memory, and Cognition*, 21(1): 116-133.

Adilson E. Motter et al. 2002. Topology of the conceptual network of language. *Physical Review E*, 65.

Roberto Navigli and Mirella Lapata. 2007. Graph Connectivity Measures for Unsupervised Word Sense Disambiguation. In *Proceedings of the 20th International Joint Conference on Artificial Intelligence*.

Douglas L. Nelson, Vanesa M. McKinney, Nancy R. Gee, and Gerson A. Janczura. 1998. Interpreting the influence of implicitly activated memories on recall and recognition. *Psychological Review*, 105:299-324.

Mariano Sigman and Guillermo A. Cecchi. 2002. Global organization of the WordNet lexicon. *Proceedings of the National Academy of Sciences of the United States of America*, 99(3).

Ravi Sinha and Rada Mihalcea. 2007. Unsupervised Graph-based Word Sense Disambiguation Using Measures of Word Semantic Similarity. In *Proceedings of the IEEE International Conference on Semantic Computing (ICSC 2007)*.

Jeffrey M. Siskind. 1996. A computational study of cross-situational techniques for learning word-to-meaning mappings. *Cognition*, 61(1): 1-38.

M. Medeiros Soares, G. Corso, and L. S. Lucena. 2005. The network of syllables in Portuguese. *Physica A: Statistical Mechanics and its Applications*, 355(2-4): 678-684.

Mark Steyvers and Joshua B. Tenenbaum. 2005. The Large-Scale Structure of Semantic Networks: Statistical Analyses and a Model of Semantic Growth. *Cognitive Science: A Multidisciplinary Journal*, 29(1): 41-78.

Cynthia K. Thompson. 2003. Unaccusative verb production in agrammatic aphasia: the argument structure complexity hypothesis. *Journal of Neurolinguistics*, 16(2-3).

Cynthia K. Thompson, Lewis P. Shapiro and Swathi Kiran and Jana Sobecks. 2003. The Role of Syntactic Complexity in Treatment of Sentence Deficits in Agrammatic Aphasia: The Complexity Account of Treatment Efficacy (CATE). *Journal of Speech, Language, and Hearing Research*, 46(3): 591-607.

Lauren Tonietto. 2009. *Desenvolvimento da convencionalidade e especificidade na aquisição de verbos: relações com complexidade sintática e categorização*. Ph.D. thesis, Federal University of Rio Grande do Sul.

Lauren Tonietto, Aline Villavicencio, Maity Siqueira, Maria Alice de Mattos Pimenta Parente, Tania Mara Sperb. 2008. A especificidade semântica como fator determinante na aquisição de verbos. *Psico*, 39(3): 343-351.

Duncan J. Watts and Steven H. Strogatz. 1998. Collective dynamics of 'small-world' networks. *Nature*, 6684(393):440-442.

Fei Xu and Joshua B. Tenenbaum. 2007. Word learning as Bayesian inference. *Psychological Review*, 114(2): 245-272.

Chen Yu. 2005. The emergence of links between lexical acquisition and object categorization: A computational study. *Connection Science*, 17(3-4): 381-397.

Chen Yu. 2006. Learning syntax–semantics mappings to bootstrap word learning. In *Proceedings of the 28th Conference of the Cognitive Science Society*.

Acquiring Human-like Feature-Based Conceptual Representations from Corpora

Colin Kelly
Computer Laboratory
University of Cambridge
Cambridge, CB3 0FD, UK
colin.kelly
@cl.cam.ac.uk

Barry Devereux
Centre for Speech,
Language, and the Brain
University of Cambridge
Cambridge, CB2 3EB, UK
barry@csl.psychol.cam.ac.uk

Anna Korhonen
Computer Laboratory
University of Cambridge
Cambridge, CB3 0FD, UK
anna.korhonen
@cl.cam.ac.uk

Abstract

The automatic acquisition of feature-based conceptual representations from text corpora can be challenging, given the unconstrained nature of human-generated features. We examine large-scale extraction of concept-relation-feature triples and the utility of syntactic, semantic, and encyclopedic information in guiding this complex task. Methods traditionally employed do not investigate the full range of triples occurring in human-generated norms (e.g. *flute produce sound*), rather targeting concept-feature pairs (e.g. *flute – sound*) or triples involving specific relations (e.g. *is-a*, *part-of*). We introduce a novel method that extracts candidate triples (e.g. *deer have antlers*, *flute produce sound*) from parsed data and re-ranks them using semantic information. We apply this technique to Wikipedia and the British National Corpus and assess its accuracy in a variety of ways. Our work demonstrates the utility of external knowledge in guiding feature extraction, and suggests a number of avenues for future work.

1 Introduction

In the cognitive sciences, theories about how concrete concepts such as ELEPHANT are represented in the mind have often adopted a distributed, feature-based model of conceptual knowledge (e.g. Randall et al. (2004), Tyler et al. (2000)). According to such accounts, conceptual representations consist of patterns of activation over sets of interconnected semantic feature nodes (e.g. *has_eyes*, *has_ears*, *is_large*). To test these theories empirically, cognitive psychologists require an accurate estimate of the kinds of knowledge that people are likely to represent in such a system. To date, the most important sources of such knowledge are property-norming studies, where a large number of participants write down lists of features for concepts. For example, McRae et al. (2005) collected a set of norms listing features for 541 concrete concepts. In that study, the features listed by different participants were normalised by mapping different feature descriptions with identical meanings to the same feature label.[1] Table 1 gives the ten most frequent normed features for two concepts in the norms.

elephant		banana	
Relation	*Feature*	*Relation*	*Feature*
is	large	is	yellow
has	a trunk	is	a fruit
is	an animal	is	edible
is	grey	is	soft
lives	in Africa	grows on	trees
has	ears	eaten by	peeling
has	tusks	-	grows
has	legs	eaten by	monkeys
has	four legs	is	long
has	large ears	tastes	good

Table 1: Sample triples from McRae Norms

However, property norm data have certain weaknesses (these have been widely discussed; e.g. Murphy (2002), McRae et al. (2005)). One issue is that participants tend to under-report features that are present in many of the concepts in a given category (McRae et al., 2005; Murphy, 2002). For example, for the concept ELEPHANT, participants list salient features like *has_trunk*, but not less salient features such as *breathes_air*, even though presumably all McRae et al.'s participants knew that elephants breathe air. Although the largest collection

[1]For example, for CAR, "used for transportation" and "people use it for transportation" were mapped to the same *used_for_transportation* feature.

Proceedings of the NAACL HLT 2010 First Workshop on Computational Neurolinguistics, pages 61–69,
Los Angeles, California, June 2010.

of norms lists features for over 500 concepts, the relatively small size of property norm sets still gives cause for concern. Larger sets of norms would be useful to psycholinguists; however, large-scale property norming studies are time-consuming and costly.

In NLP, researchers have developed methods for extracting and classifying generic relationships from data, e.g. Pantel and Pennacchiotti (2008), Davidov and Rappoport (2008a, 2008b). In recent years, researchers have also begun to develop methods which can automatically extract feature norm-like representations from corpora, e.g. Almuhareb and Poesio (2005), Barbu (2008), Baroni et al. (2009). The automatic approach is capable of gathering large-scale distributional data, and furthermore it is cost-effective. Corpora contain natural-language instances of words denoting concepts and their features, and therefore serve as ideal material for feature generation tasks. However, current methods are restricted to specific relations between concepts and their features, or target concept-feature pairs only. For example, Almuhareb and Poesio (2005) proposed a method based on manually developed lexico-syntactic patterns that extracts information about attributes and values of concepts. They used these syntactic patterns and two grammatical relations to create descriptions of nouns consisting of vector entries and evaluated their approach based on how well their vector descriptions clustered concepts. This method performed well, but targeted *is-a* and *part-of* relations only. Barbu (2008) combined manually defined linguistic patterns with a co-occurrence based method to extract features involving six classes of relations. He then split learning for the property classes into two distinct paradigms. One used a pattern-based approach (four classes) with a seeded pattern-learning algorithm. The other measured strength of association between the concept and referring adjectives and verbs (two classes). His pattern-based approach worked well for properties in the *superordinate* class, had reasonable recall for *stuff* and *location* classes, but zero recall for *part* class. His approach for the other two classes used various association measures which he summed to establish an overall score for potential properties.

The recent Strudel model (Baroni et al., 2009) relies on more general linguistic patterns, "connector patterns", consisting of sequences of part-of-speech (POS) tags to look for candidate feature terms near a target concept. The method assumes that "the variety of patterns connecting a concept and a potential property is a good indicator of the presence of a true semantic link". Thus, properties are scored based on the count of distinct patterns connecting them to a concept. When evaluated against the ESSLLI dataset (Baroni et al. (2008); see section 3.1), Strudel yields a precision of 23.9% – this figure is the best state-of-the-art result for unconstrained acquisition of concept-feature pairs.

It seems unlikely that further development of the shallow connector patterns will significantly improve accuracy, as these already broadly cover most POS sequences that are concept-feature connectors. Because of the difficult nature of the task, we believe that extraction of more accurate representations necessitates additional linguistic and world knowledge. Furthermore, the utility of Strudel is limited because it only produces concept-feature pairs, and not concept-relation-feature triples similar to those in human generated norms (although the distribution of the connector patterns for a extracted pair does offer clues about the broad class of semantic relation that holds between concept and feature).

In this paper, we explore issues of both methodology and evaluation that arise when attempting unconstrained, large-scale extraction of concept-relation-feature triples in corpus data. Extracting such human-like features is difficult, and we do not anticipate a high level of accuracy in these early experiments. We examine the utility of three types of external knowledge in guiding feature extraction: syntactic, semantic and encyclopedic. We build three automatically parsed corpora, two from Wikipedia and one from the British National Corpus. We introduce a method that (i) extracts concept-relation-feature triples from grammatical dependency paths produced by a parser and (ii) uses probabilistic information about semantic classes of features and concepts to re-rank the candidate triples before filtering them. We then assess the accuracy of our model using several different methods, and demonstrate that external knowledge can help guide the extraction of human-like features. Finally, we highlight issues in both methodology and evaluation that are important for further progress in this area of research.

2 Extraction Method

2.1 Corpora

We used Wikipedia to investigate the usefulness of world knowledge for our task. Almost all concepts in the McRae norms have their own Wikipedia articles, and the articles often include facts similar to those elicited in norming studies.[2] Extraneous data were removed from the articles (e.g. infoboxes, bibliographies) to create a plaintext version of each article. The 1.84 million articles were then compiled into two subcorpora. The first of these (Wiki500) consists of the Wikipedia articles corresponding to each of the McRae concepts. It contains *c.* 500 articles (1.1 million words). The second subcorpus is comprised of those articles where the title is fewer than five words long and contains one of the McRae concept words.[3] This corpus, called Wiki110K, holds 109,648 plaintext articles (36.5 million words).

We also employ the 100-million word British National Corpus (BNC) (Leech et al., 1994) which contains written (90%) and spoken (10%) English. It was designed to represent a broad cross-section of modern British English. This corpus provides an interesting contrast with Wikipedia, since we assume that any features contained in such a wide-ranging corpus would be presented in an incidental fashion rather than explicitly. The BNC may contain useful features which are encoded in everyday speech and text but not in Wikipedia, perhaps due to their ambiguity for encyclopedic purposes, or due to their non-scientific but rather common-sense nature. For example, *eaten by monkeys* is listed as a feature of BANANA in the McRae norms, but the word *monkey* does not appear in the Wikipedia *banana* article.

2.2 Candidate feature extraction

Using a modified, British English version of the published norms, we recoded them to a uniform *concept-relation-feature* representation suitable for our experiments – it is triples of this form that we aim to extract. Our method for extracting concept-relation-feature triples consists of two main stages. In the first stage, we extract large sets of candidate concept-relation-feature triples for each target concept from parsed corpus data. In the second stage, we re-rank and filter these triples with the intention of retaining only those triples which are likely to be true semantic features.

In the first stage, the corpora are parsed using the Robust Accurate Statistical Parsing (RASP) system (Briscoe et al., 2006). For each sentence in the corpora, this yields the most probable analysis returned by the parser in the form of a set of grammatical relations (GRs). The GR sets for each sentence containing the target concept noun are then retrieved from the corpus. These GRs form an undirected acyclic graph, whose nodes are labelled with words in the sentence and their POS, and whose edges are labelled with the GR types linking the nodes together. Using this graph we generate all possible paths which are rooted at our target concept node using a breadth-first search.

We then examine whether any of these paths match prototypical feature-relation GR structures according to our manually-generated rules. The rules were created by first extracting features from the McRae norms for a small subset of the concepts and extracting those sentences from the Wiki500 corpus which contained both concept and feature terms. For each sentence, we then examined each path through the graph (containing the GRs and POS tags) linking the concept, the feature, and all intermediate terms, and (providing no other rule already generated the concept-relation-feature triple) manually generated a rule based on each path.

For example, the sentence *There are also aprons that will cover the sleeves* should yield the triple *apron cover sleeve*. We examine the tree structure of the sentence rooted at the concept (*apron*):

```
apron+s:17_NN2
cmod-that cover:34_VV0
     L--- dobj sleeve+s:44_NN2
          L--- det the:40_AT
     L--- aux will:29_VM
cmod-that cover:34_VV0
xcomp be+:8_VBR
     L--- ncmod also:12_RR
     L--- ncsubj There:2_EX
```

Here, the relation is relatively simple – we merely

[2] e.g. The article *Elephant* describes how elephants are large, are mammals, and live in Africa.

[3] This was done in order to avoid articles on very specific topics which are unlikely to contain basic information about the target concept.

create a rule which requires that the relation is a verb (i.e. has a `V` POS tag), the feature has an `NN` tag and that there is a `dobj` GR linking the feature to the concept. Our rules are effectively a constraint on (a) which paths should be followed through the tree, and (b) which items in that path should be noted in our concept-relation-feature triple. By creating several such rules and applying them to a large number of sentences, we extract potential features and relations for our concepts.

We avoided specifying too many POS tags and GRs in rules since this could have resulted in too few matching paths. In the above example, we could have required also a `cmod-that` relation linking the feature and concept – but this would have excluded sentences like *the apron covered the sleeves*. Conversely, we avoided making our rules too permissive. For example, eliminating the `dobj` requirement would have yielded the triple *apron be steel* from the sentence *the apron hooks were steel.*

The application of this method to a number of concepts in the Wiki500 corpus yielded 15 rules which we employed in our experiments. We extract triples using both singular and plural occurrences of both the concept term and the feature term. We show the first three of our rules in Table 2. The first stage of our method uses the 15 rules to extract a very large number of candidate triples from corpus data.

Rule:	relation of concept has a VVN tag, feature has a NN tag and they are linked by an xcomp GR
S:	*This is an* ***anchor*** *which relies solely on being a heavy weight.*
T:	anchor be weight
Rule:	relation of concept is a verb, feature is an adjective and they are linked by an xcomp GR
S:	*Sliced* ***apples*** *turn brown with exposure to air due to the conversion of natural phenolic substances into melanin upon exposure to oxygen.*
T:	apple turn brown
Rule:	feature of concept has a VV0 tag, relation is a verb and they are linked by an aux GR
S:	*Grassy bottoms may be good holding, but only if the* ***anchor*** *can penetrate the foliage.*
T:	anchor can penetrate

Table 2: Three sample rules for a given **concept**, with example sentence (S) and corresponding triple (T).

2.3 Re-ranking based on semantic information

The second stage of our method evaluates the quality of the extracted candidates using semantic information, with the aim of filtering out the poor quality features generated in the first stage. We would expect the number of times a triple is extracted for a given concept to be proportional to the likelihood that the triple represents a true feature of that concept. However, production frequency alone is not a sufficient indicator of quality, because concept terms can produce unexpected candidate feature terms.[4]

One may attempt to address this issue by introducing semantic categories. In other words, the probability of a feature being part of a concept's representation is dependent on the semantic category to which the concept belongs (for example, *used_for-cutting* would be expected to have low probability for animal concepts). We analysed the norms to quantify this type of semantic information with the aim of identifying higher-order structure in the distribution of semantic classes for features and concepts. The overarching goal was to determine whether this information can indeed improve the accuracy of feature extraction.

In formal terms, we assume that there is a 2-dimensional probability distribution over concept and feature classes, $P(C,F)$, where C is a concept class (e.g. *Apparel*) and F is a feature class (e.g. *Materials*). Knowing this distribution provides us with a means of assessing how likely it is that a candidate feature f is true for a concept c, assuming that we know that $c \in C$ and $f \in F$. The McRae norms may be considered to be a sample drawn from this distribution, if the concept and feature terms appearing in the norms can be assigned to suitable concept and feature classes. These classes were identified by way of clustering. The reranking step employed the McRae norms so we could establish an upper bound for the semantic analysis, although we could also use other knowledge resources, e.g. the Open Mind Common Sense database (Singh et al., 2002).

2.3.1 Clustering

We utilised Lin's similarity measure (1998) for our similarity metric, employing WordNet (Fell-

[4]For example, one of the extracted triples for TIGER is *tiger have squadron* because of the RAF squadron called the Tigers.

k-means		
banjo	biscuit	blackbird
bat	cup	ox
beehive	kettle	peacock
birch	sailboat	prawn
bookcase	shoe	prune
NMF		
ashtray	bouquet	eel
bayonet	cabinet	grapefruit
cape	card	guppy
cat	cellar	moose
catfish	chandelier	otter
Hierarchical		
Fruit/Veg	*Apparel*	*Instruments*
apple	apron	accordion
avocado	armour	bagpipes
banana	belt	banjo
beehive	blouse	cello
blueberry	boot	clarinet

Table 3: First five elements alphabetically from three sample clusters for the three clustering methods.

baum, 1998) as the basis for calculating similarity. This metric is suitable for our task as we would like to generate appropriate superordinate classes for which we can calculate distributional statistics. We could merely cluster on the most frequent sense of concept and feature words in WordNet, but the most frequent sense in WordNet may not correspond to the intended sense in our feature norm data.[5] So we consider also other senses of words in WordNet by employing a manually-annotated list to choose the correct sense in WordNet. This is only possible for concept clustering since we don't possess a manual WordNet sense annotation for the 7000 McRae features; for the feature clustering, we simply use the most frequent sense in WordNet.

The concepts and feature-head terms appearing in the recoded norms were each clustered independently into 50 clusters using three methods: hierarchical clustering, *k*-means clustering and non-negative matrix factorization (NMF). We show the first five alphabetical elements from three of the clusters produced by our clustering methods in Table 3. The hierarchical clustering seems to be producing

[5] e.g. the first and second most frequent definitions of *kite* refer to a slang meaning for the word *cheque* – only the third most frequent meaning refers to *kite* as a toy, which most people would understand to be its predominant sense.

Hierarchical Clustering		
Plant Parts	*Materials*	*Activities*
berry	cotton	annoying
bush	fibre	listening
core	nylon	music
plant	silk	showing
seed	spandex	looking

Table 4: Example members of feature clusters for hierarchical clustering.

	Fruit/Veg	Apparel	Instruments
Plant Parts	0.144	0.037	0.008
Materials	0.006	0.148	0.008
Activities	0.009	0.074	0.161

Table 5: $P(F|C)$ for $C \in$ {Fruit/Veg, Apparel, Instruments} and $F \in$ {Plant Parts, Materials, Activities}

the most intuitive clusters.

We calculated the conditional probability $P(F|C)$ of a feature cluster given a concept cluster using the data in the McRae norms. Table 5 gives the conditional probability for each of the three feature clusters given each of the three concept clusters that were presented in Tables 3 and 4 for hierarchical clustering. For example, $P(\mathit{Materials}|\mathit{Apparel})$ is higher than $P(\mathit{Materials}|\mathit{Fruit/Veg})$: given a concept in the *Apparel* cluster the probability of a *Materials* feature is relatively high whereas given a concept in the *Fruit/Veg* cluster the probability of a *Materials* feature is low. The cluster analysis therefore supports our hypothesis that the likelihood of a particular feature for a particular concept is dependent on the semantic categories that both belong to.

2.3.2 Reranking

We investigated whether this distributional semantic information could be used to improve the quality of the candidate triples, by using the conditional probabilities of the appropriate feature cluster given the concept cluster as a weighting factor. To obtain the probabilities for a triple, we first find the clusters that the concept and feature-head words belong to. If the feature-head word of the extracted triple appears in the norms, its cluster membership is drawn directly from there; if not, we assign the feature-head to the feature cluster with which it has the highest average similarity.[6] Having determined the concept and fea-

[6] We use average-linkage for hiearchical and *k*-means clustering, and mean cosine similarity for NMF.

ture clusters for the triple, we reweight its raw corpus occurrence frequency by multiplying it by the conditional probability. In this way, incorrect triples that occur frequently in the data are downgraded and more plausible triples have their ranking boosted.

2.3.3 Baseline model

We also implemented as a baseline a co-occurrence-based model, based on the "SVD" model described by Baroni and colleagues (Baroni and Lenci, 2008; Baroni et al., 2009) – it is a simple, word-association method, not tailored to extracting features. A context-word-by-target-word frequency co-occurrence matrix was constructed for both corpora, with a sentence-sized window. Context words and target words were defined to be the 5,000 and 10,000 most frequent content words in the corpus respectively. The target words were supplemented with the concept words from the recoded norms. The co-occurrence matrix was reduced to 150 dimensions by singular value decomposition, and cosine similarity between pairs of target words was calculated. The 200 most similar target words to each concept acted as the feature-head terms extracted by this model.

3 Experimental Evaluation

3.1 Methods of Evaluation

We considered a number of methods for evaluating the quality of the extracted feature triples. One possibility would be to calculate precision and recall for the extracted triples with respect to the McRae norms "gold standard". However, direct comparison with the recoded norms is problematic, since there may be extracted features which are semantically equivalent to a triple in the norms but possessing a different lexical form.[7]

Since semantically identical features can be lexically different, we followed the approach taken in the ESSLLI 2008 Workshop on semantic models (Baroni et al., 2008). The gold standard for the ESSLLI task was the top 10 features for 44 of the McRae concepts. For each concept-feature pair an expansion set was generated containing synonyms of the feature terms appearing in the norms. For example, the feature *lives on water* was expanded to the set {*aquatic*, *lake*, *ocean*, *river*, *sea*, *water*}.

We would expect to find in corpus data correct features that do not appear in our "gold standard" (e.g. *breathes_air* is listed for WHALE but for no other animal). We therefore aim to attain high recall when evaluating against the ESSLLI set (since ideally all features in the norms should be extracted) but we are somewhat less concerned about achieving high precision (since extracted features that are not in the norms may still be correct, e.g. *breathes_air* for TIGER). To evaluate the ability of our model to generate such novel features, we also conducted a manual evaluation of the highest-ranked extracted features that did not appear in the norms.

Extraction set	Corpus	Prec.	Recall
SVD Baseline	Wiki500	0.0235	0.4712
	Wiki110K	0.0140	0.2798
	BNC	0.0131	0.2621
Method - unfiltered	Wiki500	0.0242	0.6515
	Wiki110K	0.0039	0.8944
	BNC	0.0042	0.8813
Method - top 20 (unweighted)	Wiki500	0.1159	0.2326
	Wiki110K	0.0761	0.1523
	BNC	0.0841	0.1692
Method - top 20 (hierarchical clustering)	Wiki500	0.1693	0.3394
	Wiki110K	0.1733	0.3553
	BNC	0.1943	0.3896
Method - top 20 (*k*-means clustering)	Wiki500	0.1159	0.2323
	Wiki110K	0.1000	0.2008
	BNC	0.1216	0.2442
Method - top 20 (NMF clustering)	Wiki500	0.1375	0.2755
	Wiki110K	0.1409	0.2826
	BNC	0.1500	0.3010

Table 6: Results when matching on features only.

3.2 Evaluation

Previous large-scale models of feature extraction have been evaluated on pairs rather than triples e.g. Baroni et al. (2009). Table 6 presents the results of our method when we evaluate using the feature-head term alone (i.e. in calculating precision and recall we disregard the relation verb and require only a match between the feature-head terms in the extracted triples and the recoded norms). Results for six sets of extractions are presented. The first set is the set of features extracted by the SVD baseline.

[7]For example, *avocado have stone* appears in the recoded norms whilst *avocado contain pit* is extracted by our method; direct comparison of these two triples results in *avocado contain pit* being incorrectly marked as an error.

The second set of extracted triples consists of the full set of triples extracted by our method, prior to the reweighting stage. "Top 20 unweighted" gives the results when all but the top 20 most frequently extracted triples for each concept are filtered out. Note that the filtering criteria here is raw extraction frequency, without reweighting by conditional probabilities. "Top 20 (*clustering type*)" are the corresponding results when the features are weighted by the conditional probability factors (derived from our three clustering methods) prior to filtering; that is, using the top 20 reranked features. The effectiveness of using the semantic class-based analysis data in our method can be assessed by comparing the filtered results with and without feature weighting.

For the baseline implementation, the results are better when we use the smaller Wiki500 corpus compared to the larger Wiki110K corpus. This is not surprising, since the smaller corpus contains only those articles which correspond to the concepts found in the norms. This smaller corpus thus minimises noise due to phenomena such as word polysemy which are more apparent in the larger corpus.

The results for the baseline model and the unfiltered method are quite similar for the Wiki500 corpus, whilst the results for the unfiltered method using the Wiki110K corpus give the maximum recall achieved by our method; 89.4% of the features are extracted, although this figure is closely followed by that of the BNC at 88.1%. As the unfiltered method is deliberately greedy, a large number of features are being extracted and therefore precision is low.

Extraction set	Corpus	Prec.	Recall
Method - top 20	Wiki500	0.1011	0.2028
(hierarchical	Wiki110K	0.1102	0.2210
clustering)	BNC	0.0955	0.1917

Table 7: Results for our best method when matching on features and relations.

For the results of the filtered method, where all but the top 20 of features were discarded, we see the benefit of reranking, with the reranked frequencies for all three clustering types yielding much higher precision and recall scores than the unweighted method. Our best performance is achieved using the BNC and hierarchical clustering, where we obtain 19.4% precision and 38.9% recall. Thus both general and encyclopedic corpus data prove useful for the task. An interesting question is whether these two data types offer different, complementary feature types for the task. We discuss this point further in section 3.3.

Using exactly the same gold standard, Baroni et al. (2009) obtained precision of 23.9%. However, this result is not directly comparable with ours, since we define precision over the whole set of extracted features while Baroni et al. considered the top 10 extracted features only.

The innovation of our method is that it uses information about the GR-graph of the sentence to also extract the relation which appears in the path linking the concept and feature terms in the sentence, which is not possible in a purely co-occurrence-based model. We therefore also evaluated the extracted triples using the full relation + feature-head pair (i.e. both the feature and the relation verb have to be correct). The results for our best method are shown in Table 7. Unsurprisingly, because this task is more difficult, precision and recall are reduced. However, since we enforce no constraints on what the relation may be and since we do not have expanded synonym sets for our relations (as we do for our features) it is actually impressive to have both the exact relation verb and feature matching with the recoded norms almost one in every five times. To our knowledge, our work is the first to try to compare extracted features to the full relation and feature norm parts of the triple.

3.3 Qualitative analysis

Since a key aim of our work is to learn novel features in corpus data, we also performed a qualitative evaluation of the extracted features and relations. This analysis revealed that many of the errors were not true errors but potentially valid triples missing from the gold standard. Table 8 shows the top 10 features for two concepts extracted by our best method from the Wiki500 corpus and the BNC corpus. We label those features that are correct according to the norms as Correct (C), those which do not appear in our norms but we believe to be plausible as Plausible (P), and those that do not appear in the norms and are also implausible as Incorrect (I). We can see that our method has detected several plausible features not appearing in the norms (and thus our gold standard), e.g. *swan have chick* and *screwdriver be*

swan					
Wiki500			BNC		
be	bird	C	have	number	I
be	black	P	have	water	C
have	chick	P	have	lake	C
have	plumage	C	be	bird	C
have	feather	C	be	white	C
restrict	water	C	have	neck	C
be	mute	P	be	wild	P
eat	grass	P	have	duck	I
turn	elisa	I	have	song	I
have	neck	C	have	pair	I
screwdriver					
Wiki500			BNC		
use	handle	C	have	tool	C
have	blade	P	have	end	P
use	tool	C	have	blade	P
remedy	problem	P	have	hand	I
have	size	P	be	sharp	P
have	head	C	have	bit	P
rotate	end	P	have	arm	I
have	plastic	P	be	large	P
achieve	goal	I	be	sonic	P
have	hand	I	have	range	P

Table 8: Top 10 returned features and relations for *swan* and *screwdriver*.

sharp. Indeed, it could be argued that some 'incorrect' features (e.g. *screwdriver achieve goal*) could be considered to be at least broadly accurate. We recognise that the ideal evaluation for our method would involve having human participants assess the extracted features for a diverse cross-section of our concepts, but this is beyond the scope of this paper.

When considering the top 20 features extracted using our best method applied to the Wiki500 corpus versus the BNC corpus, the overlap of features is relatively low at 22.73%. When one also takes the extracted relations into account, this figure descends to 6.45%. It is clear that relatively distinct groups of features are being extracted from the encyclopedic and general corpus data. Future work could investigate combining these for improved performance e.g. using the intersection of the best features from the BNC and Wiki110k corpora to improve precision and the union to improve recall.

4 Discussion

This paper examined large-scale, unconstrained acquisition of human-like feature norms from corpus data. Our work was not limited to only a subset of concepts, relation types or concept-feature pairs. Rather, we investigated concepts, features and relations in conjunction, and extracted property norm-like concept-relation-feature triples.

Our investigation shows that external knowledge is highly useful in guiding this challenging task. Encyclopedic information proved useful for feature extraction: although our Wikipedia corpora are considerably smaller than the BNC, they performed almost equally well. We also demonstrated the benefits of employing syntactic information in feature extraction: our base extraction method operating on parsed data outperforms the co-occurrence-based baseline and permits us to extract relation verbs. This underscores the usefulness of parsing for semantically meaningful feature extraction. This is consistent with recent work in the field of computational lexical semantics, although GR data has not previously been successfully applied to feature extraction.

We showed that semantic information about co-occurring concept and feature clusters can be used to enhance feature acquisition. We employed the McRae norms for our analysis, however we could also employ other knowledge resources and cluster relation verbs using recent methods, e.g. Sun and Korhonen (2009), Vlachos et al. (2009).

Our paper has also investigated methods of evaluation, which is a critical but difficult issue for feature extraction. Most recent approaches have been evaluated against the ESSLLI sub-set of the McRae norms which expands the set of features in the norms with their synonyms. Yet even expansion sets like the ESSLLI norms do not facilitate adequate evaluation because they are not complete in the sense that there are true features which are not included in the norms. Our qualitative analysis shows that many of the errors against the recoded norms are in fact correct or plausible features. Future work can aim for larger-scale qualitative evaluation using multiple judges as well as investigating other task-based evaluations. For example, we have demonstrated that our automatically-acquired feature representations can make predictions about fMRI activity associated with concept stimuli that are as powerful as those produced by a manually-selected set of features (Devereux et al., 2010).

Acknowledgments

This research was supported by EPSRC grant EP/F030061/1 and the Royal Society University Research Fellowship, UK. We are grateful to McRae and colleagues for making their norms publicly available, and to the anonymous reviewers for their input.

References

Abdulrahman Almuhareb and Massimo Poesio. 2005. Concept learning and categorization from the web. In *Proceedings of the 27th Annual Meeting of the Cognitive Science Society*, pages 103–108.

Eduard Barbu. 2008. Combining methods to learn feature-norm-like concept descriptions. In *Proceedings of the ESSLLI Workshop on Distributional Lexical Semantics*, pages 9–16.

Marco Baroni and Alessandro Lenci. 2008. Concepts and properties in word spaces. *Italian Journal of Linguistics*, 20(1):55–88.

Marco Baroni, Stefan Evert, and Alessandro Lenci, editors. 2008. *ESSLLI 2008 Workshop on Distributional Lexical Semantics*.

Marco Baroni, Brian Murphy, Eduard Barbu, and Massimo Poesio. 2009. Strudel: A corpus-based semantic model based on properties and types. *Cognitive Science*, pages 1–33.

Edward J. Briscoe, John Carroll, and Rebecca Watson. 2006. The second release of the RASP system. In *Proceedings of the Interactive Demo Session of COLING/ACL-06*, pages 77–80.

D. Davidov and A. Rappoport. 2008a. Classification of semantic relationships between nominals using pattern clusters. *ACL.08*.

D. Davidov and A. Rappoport. 2008b. Unsupervised discovery of generic relationships using pattern clusters and its evaluation by automatically generated SAT analogy questions. *ACL.08*.

Barry Devereux, Colin Kelly, and Anna Korhonen. 2010. Using fmri activation to conceptual stimuli to evaluate methods for extracting conceptual representations from corpora. In *Proceedings of the NAACL-HLT Workshop on Computational Neurolinguistics*.

Christiane Fellbaum, editor. 1998. *WordNet: An electronic lexical database*. MIT Press.

G. Leech, R. Garside, and M. Bryant. 1994. CLAWS4: the tagging of the British National Corpus. In *Proceedings of the 15th conference on Computational linguistics-Volume 1*, pages 622–628.

Dekang Lin. 1998. An information-theoretic definition of similarity. In *Proceedings of ICML'98*, pages 296–304.

Ken McRae, George S. Cree, Mark S. Seidenberg, and Chris McNorgan. 2005. Semantic feature production norms for a large set of living and nonliving things. *Behavior Research Methods*, 37:547–559.

Gregory Murphy. 2002. *The big book of concepts*. The MIT Press, Cambridge, MA.

Patrick Pantel and Marco Pennacchiotti. 2008. Automatically harvesting and ontologizing semantic relations. In Paul Buitelaar and Philipp Cimiano, editors, *Ontology learning and population*. IOS press.

Billi Randall, Helen E. Moss, Jennifer M. Rodd, Mike Greer, and Lorraine K. Tyler. 2004. Distinctiveness and correlation in conceptual structure: Behavioral and computational studies. *Journal of Experimental Psychology: Learning, Memory & Cognition*, 30(2):393–406.

P. Singh, T. Lin, E. Mueller, G. Lim, T. Perkins, and W. Li Zhu. 2002. Open Mind Common Sense: Knowledge acquisition from the general public. *On the Move to Meaningful Internet Systems 2002: CoopIS, DOA, and ODBASE*, pages 1223–1237.

Lin Sun and Anna Korhonen. 2009. Improving Verb Clustering with Automatically Acquired Selectional Preferences. *Empirical Methods on Natural Language Processing*.

L. K. Tyler, H. E. Moss, M. R. Durrant-Peatfield, and J. P. Levy. 2000. Conceptual structure and the structure of concepts: A distributed account of category-specific deficits. *Brain and Language*, 75(2):195–231.

Andreas Vlachos, Anna Korhonen, and Zoubin Ghahramani. 2009. Unsupervised and constrained dirichlet process mixture models for verb clustering. In *Proceedings of the Workshop on Geometrical Models of Natural Language Semantics*, pages 74–82, Athens, Greece.

Using fMRI activation to conceptual stimuli to evaluate methods for extracting conceptual representations from corpora

Barry Devereux
Centre for Speech, Language and the Brain
Department of Experimental Psychology
University of Cambridge
barry@csl.psychol.cam.ac.uk

Colin Kelly & Anna Korhonen
Computer Laboratory
University of Cambridge
{ck329,alk23}@cam.ac.uk

Abstract

We present a series of methods for deriving conceptual representations from corpora and investigate the usefulness of the fMRI data and machine learning methodology of Mitchell et al. (2008) as a basis for evaluating the different models. Within this framework, the quality of a semantic model is quantified by its ability to predict the fMRI activation associated with conceptual stimuli. Mitchell et al. used a manually-acquired set of verbs as the basis for their semantic model; in this paper, we also consider automatically acquired feature-norm-like semantic representations. These models make different assumptions about the kinds of information available in corpora that is relevant to representing conceptual knowledge. Our results indicate that automatically-acquired representations can make equally powerful predictions about the brain activity associated with the stimuli.

1 Introduction

Mitchell et al. (2008) presented a novel approach for predicting human brain activity associated with conceptual stimuli. This approach represents a useful development for interdisciplinary researchers interested in lexical semantics, for several reasons. Most broadly, it is useful in testing the hypothesis that distributional properties of words in corpora can reveal important information about the meanings of words. A strong version of this hypothesis (i.e. that children in part learn the meaning of concrete concept words from co-occurring words in discourse that they are exposed to) has formed the basis of one class of probabilistic cognitive models of conceptual representation (Andrews et al., 2005; Andrews et al., 2009; Steyvers, 2010). Furthermore this approach is useful for testing hypotheses about the kind of co-occurring information that is useful for representing conceptual semantics. In Mitchell et al.'s work (2008), for example, they adopt the position that the meaning of concrete concepts is encoded in the brain with information associated with basic sensory and motor activities (such as actions involving changes to spatial relationships and physical actions performed on objects).

At a more technical level, Mitchell et al.'s fMRI activation data[1] give researchers developing feature-based models of conceptual representation an important benchmark for evaluation. For these researchers, a key problem is the lack of a reasonable "gold standard" against which the quality of the representations generated by a computational model may be evaluated. Previous research has adopted two main approaches to evaluation. Firstly, some models – especially those aiming to extract representations composed of psychologically meaningful semantic feature units, such as Baroni et al. (2009) – have been evaluated against features gathered in large scale property norming studies (e.g. McRae et al. (2005)).[2] By comparing the system output against features elicited by people, this kind of eval-

[1] fMRI data measures changes in oxygen concentrations in the brain. These changes are tied to cognitive processes.

[2] In property norming studies, a group of human subjects are asked to cite features which come to mind for a given concept. These features are compiled by frequency (with a minimum frequency cut-off) to generate a list of features for each concept.

Proceedings of the NAACL HLT 2010 First Workshop on Computational Neurolinguistics, pages 70–78,
Los Angeles, California, June 2010.

uation aims to test the psychological validity of computational methods. Furthermore, it allows a fine-grained analysis of performance, for example by revealing the classes of features (part-of, taxonomic, etc) which a given model is particularly good at extracting (Baroni et al., 2008).

However, property norms come with important caveats. One problem is that they tend to over-represent informative or salient information about concepts whilst under-representing other kinds of features. For example, participants report that camels have humps, but not that camels have hearts, even though all participants are likely to have both pieces of information accessible in their representation of the concept CAMEL. If a model is successful in extracting these less salient features, there is no way of evaluating their correctness using property norms. A related issue is that participants can only report verbalizable features, which may not represent the total sum of their conceptual knowledge (Murphy, 2002; McRae et al., 2005).

A second problem with using property norms as the basis of evaluation is that there is often no direct lexical match between feature terms appearing in the system output and the norms. Feature norms are typically normalized such that near-synonymous properties (e.g. *is endangered*, *is an endangered species*, *is almost extinct*, etc., for WHALE) given by different participants are mapped to the same feature label (e.g. *is endangered*). As a consequence, a model may correctly extract *endangered* for WHALE, but other lexical forms of the same feature will not match any feature in the norms. One solution to this is to create an expansion set for each feature which includes its synonyms (Baroni et al., 2008). However, this is only a partial solution because lexical variation in features is not limited to synonyms.

A second approach to evaluating semantic models uses classification or similarity data. For example, Andrews et al. (2009) evaluated their models by calculating cosine similarity scores between semantic representations and using these similarity scores to predict behavioral data which are contingent on the semantic similarity between pairs of concepts (e.g. lexical substitution errors, semantic priming latencies, word-association norms, etc). Although this approach is psychologically motivated, it evaluates a set of extracted features more indirectly than comparison with norm data. In computational linguistics, a similarly indirect evaluation method is to cluster the extracted representations. This approach avoids the difficulties in evaluating individual features; however it only allows consideration along one dimension of the data, namely the similarity between pairs of concepts.

fMRI data such as the Mitchell et al. (2008) dataset offers an advancement over both of these evaluation techniques. Unlike, for example, property norming data, fMRI data offers direct insight into how the brain is functioning in response to given stimuli. Its multidimensional nature makes it easier to inspect what aspects of meaning a particular model is performing strongly or weakly on, and allows for better control of experimental variation. Finally, it avoids the two major issues associated with property norms, which we outlined above.

This paper is structured as follows. In the next section, we briefly describe the models which we used to extract conceptual representations for the 60 concepts in the Mitchell et al. (2008) dataset. In Section 3, we outline our experimental objectives, and the framework we adopt for testing our semantic models. In Section 4, we present the results of our evaluation, which indicate above chance performance for each of the models. Finally, we examine the differences between models by investigating for which concepts prediction of the fMRI activity is poorest, and discuss these differences with respect to the differing assumptions made by the methods.

2 Semantic models

We consider four different semantic models in this paper, which are described briefly below. These models were selected as we were interested in the various kinds of knowledge (part-of-speech, syntactic, and semantic) in corpora available to the extraction process, and the extent to which the use of these types of knowledge can affect the quality of the extracted conceptual representations.

2.1 Mitchell verb-based semantic model

The first semantic model we considered was that of Mitchell et al. (2008). This model assumes that sensory-motor information is an important aspect of conceptual representation, and that the information relevant to a target concept's representation can be estimated from the concept word's frequency of co-occurrence with 25 sensory-motor verbs (*eat*, *manipulate*, *push*, etc) in a very large corpus. Our reimplementation of this method used the co-occurrence statistics provided by Mitchell et al.[3] which were extracted from the Google n-gram corpus consisting of 1 trillion words of web text.

2.2 SVD model

Secondly, we implemented a co-occurrence-based Singular Value Decomposition (SVD) model based on the one described by Baroni and colleagues (Baroni and Lenci, 2008; Baroni et al., 2009). This model combines aspects of both the HAL (Landauer et al., 1998) and LSA (Lund and Burgess, 1996) models in constructing representations for words based on their co-occurrences in texts. A word-by-word co-occurrence matrix was constructed for our corpus, storing how often each target word co-occurred with each context word. The set of context words consisted of the 5,000 most frequent content words (i.e. words not occurring in a stop-list of function words) appearing in the corpus. The set of target words consisted of the 60 concept terms appearing in the fMRI dataset, supplemented with the 10,000 most frequent content words in the corpus (with the exception of the top 10 most frequent words). For calculating co-occurrence frequency between target and context words, the context window was defined by sentence boundaries: two words were considered to co-occur if they appeared in the same sentence[4].

Following Baroni and Lenci (2008), the dimensionality of the target-word $\times$ context-word co-occurrence matrix was reduced to 150 columns by singular value decomposition. That is, the singular value decomposition of the co-occurrence matrix was computed and the 150 left singular vectors that accounted for most of the variance, multiplied by the corresponding singular values, were used as the 150-dimensional representation of each target term. Similarity between pairs of target words was calculated as the cosine between their vectors, and for each of the 60 concept words in the experimental stimuli we chose the 200 most similar target words to act as the feature terms extracted by the model. The corpus used with this model was the British National Corpus (BNC) (Leech et al., 1994).

[3] `http://www.cs.cmu.edu/~tom/science2008/semanticFeatureVectors.html`

[4] In Baroni et al.'s implementation a context window of 5 (Baroni and Lenci, 2008) or 20 (Baroni et al., 2009) words either side of the target word was used instead; we chose a sentence-based context window as it is analogous to the context used in our experimental method (described in the following section).

2.3 Novel extraction method

Finally we implemented a novel extraction method, which aims to extract property-norm-like, psychologically meaningful features from corpus data (Kelly et al., 2010). The method aims to extract semantically unconstrained feature triples of the form *concept-relation-feature* , where *feature* is a feature (either noun or adjective) of the target concept and *relation* is a verb representing the semantic relationship between them. Examples of extracted triples include: *swan be white*, *swan have neck* and *screwdriver be tool*. The model uses a corpus parsed for grammatical relations (GRs) using Robust Accurate Statistical Parsing (RASP) (Briscoe et al., 2006). For each sentence containing a target concept, the set of GRs for that sentence are examined to test whether they match manually-created rules. These rules include prototypical feature-relation GR structures connecting elements of the sentence and represent dependency patterns which encode potential semantic relationships between the concept and candidate feature terms occurring in the sentence. A large set of candidate triples are extracted by applying these rules to each sentence in the corpus containing a target concept, and the triples for each concept are ranked by their frequency of extraction. In the second stage of the method, the extracted triples are reweighted on the basis of probabilistic high-level semantic information obtained from human property norm data. This subsequent stage has the effect of increasing the weight associated with more high-quality features and downgrading lower-quality features. The extraction method is described more fully in Kelly et al. (2010). For this method we also used the BNC. The top 200 triples ranked by frequency (i.e. unweighted) and the top 200 features after reweighting with the semantic data were used in our experiments.

3 Experiment

As mentioned above, we are primarily interested in using the fMRI data to evaluate the quality of the different methods for extracting conceptual representations from corpora (rather than being interested in investigating methods for predicting fMRI activation). We make no attempt to build on the method described by Mitchell et al. (2008), although there are likely to be many interesting avenues through which that method could be extended.[5] We therefore followed the Mitchell et al. methodology as closely as possible, using the same multiple regression training and leave-two-out cross-validation paradigms as presented in their paper and supporting online material. The only parameter that we varied was the extraction method (and corpus) that was used to generate the feature-vectors associated with the 60 concepts that were used during the training phase. The quality of the predictions generated for the concepts using each semantic model can therefore be adopted as an index of model performance.

The Mitchell et al. method uses co-occurrence with a specific set of 25 manually selected verbs (*eat*, *push*, etc) that are the same for each concept. This results in 25-dimensional feature vectors for input into training. However, for both the SVD model and our triple extraction models there are no *a priori* constraints on the number of unique features that can be extracted for the concepts. For these models, we selected the top 200 features associated with each concept; therefore, across all 60 concepts in the Mitchell et al. dataset, there are thousands of unique features extracted which are used in the concepts' representations. To ensure that the linear regression model for each method would be fitted using the same number of free parameters during training (thereby maximizing the comparability of the different methods), we reduced the dimensionality of the generated feature spaces for the SVD method and the two triple-extraction methods using Principal Components Analysis (PCA). The concept × feature extraction frequency matrices for the three models were submitted to PCA, and the first 25 components (i.e. those components which best characterized the variance of the original features) for each model were selected. In the case of the SVD model, these 25 dimensions explained 77.7% of the variance in the original 3,061-dimensional vectors. For our unweighted extraction method, the 25 extracted components explained 63.0% of the original 5,525 dimensions; for the weighted method the components explained 71.5% of the original 6,567 dimensions.

[5] For example, the method currently makes the simplifying assumption that the activity in neighbouring voxels is independent.

Triples (weighted)		*SVD*	
PCA1	**PCA2**	**PCA1**	**PCA2**
	Highest-valued concepts		
horse	house	coat	butterfly
cat	apartment	skirt	cow
cow	dog	shirt	ant
dog	igloo	pants	bee
beetle	car	dress	lettuce
	Lowest-valued concepts		
knife	pants	car	desk
door	coat	watch	arm
hammer	dress	horse	chair
saw	skirt	dog	knife
chisel	shirt	fly	leg

Table 1: Highest- and lowest-valued concepts for the first two components for the SVD and weighted triple-extraction methods.

It is interesting to consider the kind of semantic information that is being captured by the resultant PCA components. In particular, the components appear to capture meaningful distinctions between stimuli. For example, the first PCA component for our weighted triple extraction method can be interpreted as the concepts' degree of "animalness" (animal stimuli have high values on this component). Table 1 presents the five highest and lowest-valued concepts for the first two components for the SVD model and the weighted triple extraction model. Concepts which overlap with respect to a specific set of semantic properties tend to have high or low values on a given dimension, indicating that that component is capturing a specific cluster of co-occurring semantic features. For example, PCA1 for SVD can be interpreted as "has features associated with clothing".

Therefore, a key difference between the Michell

Method	Feature Type	POS	Syntax	Semantics
Mitchell	25 verbs	no	no	no
SVD	tuples (content-words)	yes	no	no
triple-extraction method (unweighted)	feature-triples	yes	yes	no
triple-extraction method (weighted)	feature-triples	yes	yes	yes

Table 2: Comparison of the information available to each model.

et al. model and our models is that while Mitchell et al. posit that certain sensory-motor function verbs can act as important features of concepts, our models instead place more importance on intrinsic semantic features.

Finally, Table 2 gives a summary comparison of the different models, in terms of whether or not each uses part of speech (POS) data, syntactic information (i.e. GRs), and semantic filtering (Section 2.3).

It should be noted that the BNC corpus (used with the SVD model and our triple-extraction method) is 10,000 times smaller than the corpus from which the Mitchell et al. feature vectors are derived. As such the semantic representations we extract with our method need to make better use of the data available in the corpus if they are to compete with the verb-based features used by Mitchell et al.'s method.

4 Results

The accuracy for each of the four methods was evaluated using a leave-two-out validation paradigm. There are 1,770 possible pairs of concepts that can be drawn from the set of 60 concept stimuli. Training was performed separately for each participant and for each of the 1,770 held-out pairs. Given a particular participant and held-out pair, for each voxel v we fit the activation at that voxel to the set of 58 training items with multiple linear regression, using as predictor variables the elements of the 25-dimensional feature vectors associated with each of the 58 concepts. Training therefore yields a set of 25 β-coefficients, which can be used to generate a prediction for the activation y_v of voxel v for the held-out word w using the equation

$$y_v^{\text{pred}} = \sum_{i=1}^{25} \beta_{v,i} f_{i,w} \quad (1)$$

where $f_{i,w}$ is the ith element of the feature vector for word w (see Mitchell et al. (2008) for details). Over all voxels, this method gives a prediction for the activation with respect to the held-out word w which can then be compared to the observed activation for that stimulus.

Rather than comparing the activity between predicted and observed images using all voxels, we compared images using only the 500 most stable voxels for each participant. For each participant, the 500 most stable voxels were the voxels which gave the most consistent pattern of activation across the six presentations of all 60 stimuli (see Mitchell et al. (2008) for details).

The top row of Figure 1 presents the learned coefficients for one feature dimension for each of the four semantic models considered in our experiments (for these images, all voxels rather then the 500 most stable voxels are used). For the Mitchell et al. method, the coefficients presented correspond to the verb *eat*; for the other models the feature is the PCA component that explained the most variance in the original representations. We also present the predicted images for the concepts CELERY and AIRPLANE, calculated on the coefficients learned over the remaining 58 concepts. Importantly, for the Mitchell et al. method (column (a)), the learned coefficients for *eat* and the predicted images for CELERY and AIRPLANE agree with those reported by Mitchell et al. (2008, Figure 2 & online supplementary material[6]).

We calculated similarity between predicted and observed images using both cosine and Pearson correlation and the 500 most stable voxels; we report the results using Pearson correlation here as this measure consistently gave slightly better accuracies

[6] `http://www.cs.cmu.edu/~tom/science2008/featureSignaturesP1.html`

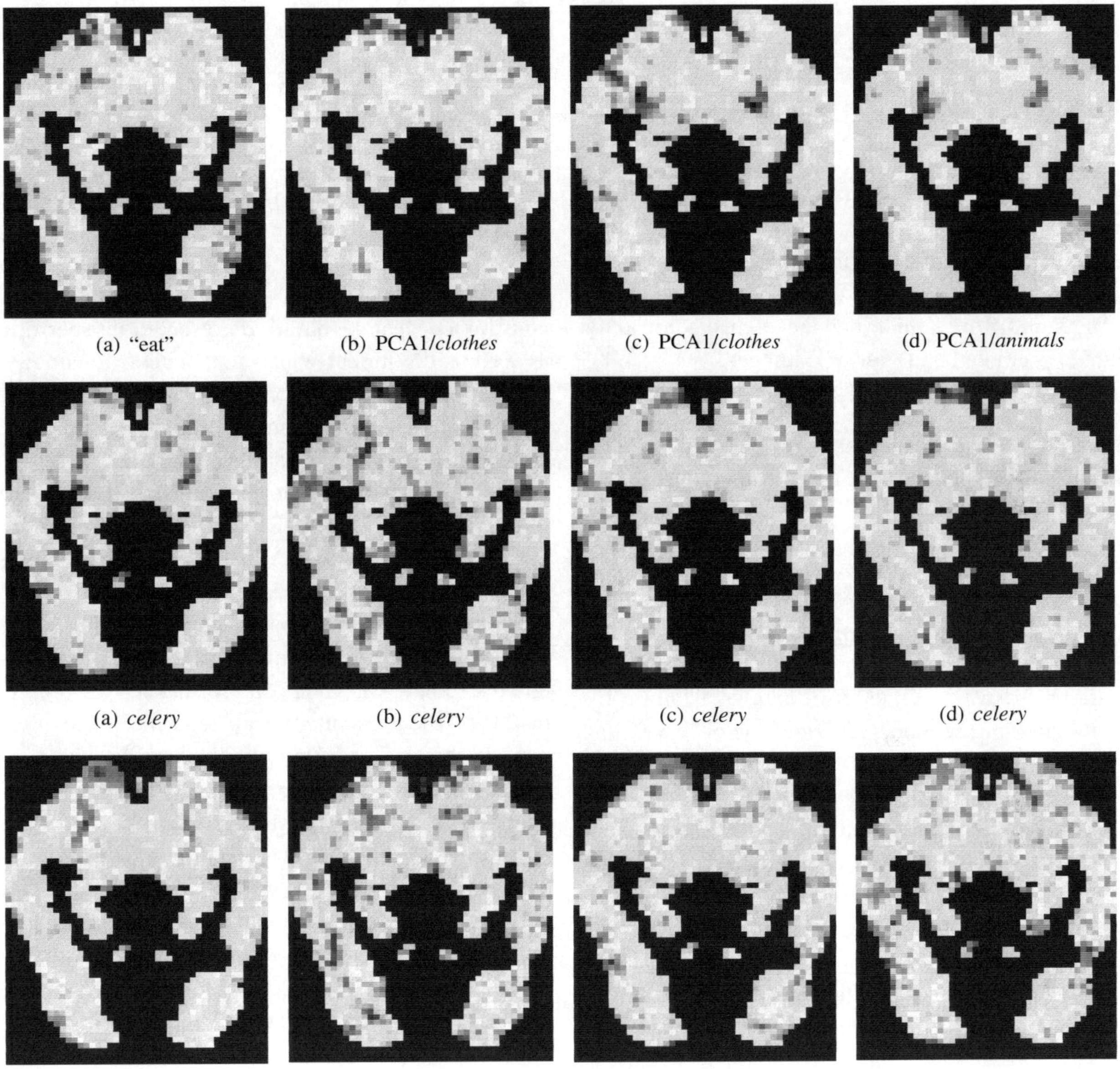

(a) "eat" (b) PCA1/*clothes* (c) PCA1/*clothes* (d) PCA1/*animals*

(a) *celery* (b) *celery* (c) *celery* (d) *celery*

(a) *airplane* (b) *airplane* (c) *airplane* (d) *airplane*

Figure 1: Learned coefficients on a selected feature dimension (top row) and predicted activation for CELERY (middle row) and AIRPLANE (bottom row) for four semantic models: (a) Mitchell et al. (2008), (b) SVD (c) triple extraction method (unweighted), and (d) triple extraction method (weighted). Warmer colours indicate higher values (i.e. larger β-coefficients for the feature dimensions and higher predicted activation for the concepts). PCA components have been given intuitive labels indicating the kind of information described by that component (see Table 1). As in Figure 2 of Mitchell et al. (2008), the figure shows just one slice in the horizontal plane (z = -12 in MNI space) for one participant (P1). The predicted images for CELERY and AIRPLANE were generated from the feature coefficients learned on the other 58 concepts using each of the four models; the corresponding observed images for CELERY and AIRPLANE can be found in Mitchell et al. (2008) Figure 2 B.

Method	P1	P2	P3	P4	P5	P6	P7	P8	P9	Mean
Mitchell et al. (2008)	0.84	0.83	0.76	0.81	0.79	0.66	0.73	0.64	0.68	0.75
SVD	0.82	0.67	0.79	0.83	0.74	0.64	0.64	0.70	0.75	0.73
Triple-extraction (unweighted)	0.82	0.71	0.79	0.80	0.70	0.69	0.65	0.53	0.78	0.72
Triple-extraction (weighted)	0.82	0.72	0.76	0.83	0.73	0.65	0.68	0.51	0.76	0.72

Table 3: Accuracy results for the four semantic models.

for each of the four models (the results are very similar using the cosine measure). Following Mitchell et al. (2008; supplementary material), a match score for each held out pair w_1 and w_2 was calculated as the sum of the similarities between the correctly aligned predicted and observed images:

$$a = sim(w_1^{\text{pred}}, w_1^{\text{obs}}) + sim(w_2^{\text{pred}}, w_2^{\text{obs}}) \quad (2)$$

Similarly a mismatch score was calculated as

$$b = sim(w_1^{\text{pred}}, w_2^{\text{obs}}) + sim(w_2^{\text{pred}}, w_1^{\text{obs}}) \quad (3)$$

Cases where the match score is greater than the mismatch score (i.e. $a > b$) count as successes for the model (i.e. the model correctly identifies the two predicted images). Otherwise there is a failure by the model (i.e. the model identifies the observed image for w_1 as being w_2 and vice-versa).

Table 3 presents the results of the leave-two-out cross-validation evaluation, giving the proportion (across all 1,770 pairs) of predicted images for the held-out pairs that were correctly matched to the observed images.[7] The original Mitchell et al. (2008) model has the best mean performance, although across the nine participants, there is no significant difference in accuracy between any of the models ($|t(8)| < 1.49$, $p > 0.17$, for all pairwise paired t-tests between Mitchell et al. (2008), SVD, and weighted triple extraction).

That there is no difference between the performance of the Mitchell et al. (2008), SVD and triple extraction methods is surprising, given the different kinds of information that are available to the different models. In particular, the models that automatically acquire very general and semantically unconstrained feature-based representations perform as well as the model which uses a set of manually-selected sensory-motor verbs, even though the representations generated for these models are derived from 10,000 times less corpus data.

As mentioned in our introduction, an advantage of evaluating against the fMRI dataset is that this multi-dimensional data allows us to investigate strengths and weaknesses of different models in a way which is not possible using similarity or clustering-based evaluation. As a very simple investigation of specific differences in model performance, we present in Table 4 the pairs of concepts for which each of the models performs most poorly on. The Mitchell et al. (2008) method appears to do poorly on pairs of concepts where a constituent word can be ambiguous with respect to its part-of-speech (e.g. SAW, BEAR). This is not surprising, given that part-of-speech data is not available in the Google n-gram corpus used with this method. The performance of the Mitchell et al. method might therefore be improved significantly by applying heuristics to the n-gram data to make inferences about the correct part-of-speech of instances of words like SAW and BEAR. For the SVD and weighted triple extraction methods, which both use the BNC corpus, there is some evidence that the models are performing poorly for relatively low frequency words[8] (e.g. CHISEL), words which are semantically ambiguous as nouns (e.g. ARM), and pairs which are semantically similar (e.g. SPOON & KNIFE). This suggests that the SVD and triple extraction methods may perform better with a larger and more diverse corpus.

[7] Our results for the Mitchell et al. (2008) method are similar, though not identical, to those reported in that paper (where the reported mean accuracy across all participants is 0.77, using cosine similarity). Our implementation of the method for selecting the 500 most stable voxels yields slightly different voxels from those obtained by Mitchell et al. (2008; see supplementary material). In any case, the same set of 500 voxels for each participant were used for generating the results of each model presented here, and so we do not believe that this discrepancy affects comparison of the different models.

[8] AIRPLANE is relatively low frequency in the BNC; it may be more sensible to use the word AEROPLANE with a British corpus.

Mitchell et al.		SVD		Triple Extraction (weighted)	
Pair	*Nr.*	*Pair*	*Nr.*	*Pair*	*Nr.*
bear saw	0	cup airplane	0	dresser chimney	0
bell carrot	0	cup lettuce	0	airplane chisel	0
bell saw	0	horse beetle	0	airplane hand	0
knife bear	0	chisel arm	0	airplane tomato	0
cup saw	1	hammer arm	1	spoon chisel	0
bear tomato	1	dresser arch	1	spoon knife	0

Table 4: Leave-out pairs for which each model performs least accurately, across the nine participants. *Nr.* = the number of participants for which this leave-out pair was correctly matched.

5 Conclusion

The fMRI dataset and training and evaluation methodology presented by Mitchell et al. (2008) gives researchers an interesting new framework with which to evaluate the quality of feature-based conceptual representations extracted from corpora. This framework avoids some of the problems inherent in evaluating extracted representations against a "gold standard" based on participant-generated property norms. It also provides a rich multi-dimensional dataset through which the strengths and weaknesses of extraction methods can be identified.

We have applied this evaluation framework to four feature extraction methods which use different sources of information available in corpora to extract conceptual representations. Surprisingly, in spite of their major differences, we did not find any significant difference in performance between the models.

This finding has interesting theoretical implications, given that previous research has suggested that aspects of meaning defined by sensory-motor verbs may have a somewhat distinctive role to play in predicting the fMRI activation associated with conceptual stimuli (Mitchell et al., 2008). Our results suggest that general feature-based representations of concepts, which place no *a priori* distinction on sensory-motor properties, may be equally capable of predicting activation to conceptual stimuli. This highlights the potential for the Mitchell et al. method to be used to inform both distributed and sensory-motor accounts of conceptual representation (e.g. McRae et al. (1997), Cree et al. (2006), Tyler et al. (2000), Tyler & Moss (2001), Moss et al. (2007), Martin & Chao (2001)), as well as providing a benchmark with which to assess semantic model development. In a similar vein, Murphy et al. (2009) used a dependency-parsed corpus yielding verb co-occurrence statistics to predict EEG[9] activation patterns with significant accuracy.

The training and evaluation framework presented by Mitchell et al. (2008) represents just one point in a large space of possibilities for using computational modelling to predict human brain activity associated with conceptual stimuli. In these initial experiments, we have chosen to follow the Mitchell et al. approach as closely as possible, in order to maximize comparability with their results. In future work, we aim to investigate other methods for training and evaluation, other corpora and other sources of imaging data. Furthermore, we aim to use the evaluation results from such work to inform the development of our extraction method.

Acknowledgments

Our work was funded by the EPSRC grant EP/F030061/1, and the Royal Society University Research Fellowship, UK. We thank Mitchell et al. (2008) and McRae et al. (2005) for making their data publically available.

References

Mark Andrews, G. Vigliocco, and D. Vinson. 2005. Integrating attributional and distributional information in a probabilistic model of meaning representation. In Timo Honkela et al., editor, *Proceedings of AKRR'05, International and Interdisciplinary Conference on Adaptive Knowledge Representation and Rea-*

[9] EEG measures voltages induced by neuronal firing across the human scalp.

soning, pages 15–25, Espoo, Finland: Helsinki University of Technology.

Mark Andrews, Gabriella Vigliocco, and David Vinson. 2009. Integrating experiential and distributional data to learn semantic representations. *Psychological Review*, 116(3):463–498.

Marco Baroni and Alessandro Lenci. 2008. Concepts and properties in word spaces. *From context to meaning: Distributional models of the lexicon in linguistics and cognitive science (Special issue of the Italian Journal of Linguistics)*, 20(1):55–88.

Marco Baroni, Stefan Evert, and Alessandro Lenci, editors. 2008. *ESSLLI 2008 Workshop on Distributional Lexical Semantics*.

Marco Baroni, Brian Murphy, Eduard Barbu, and Massimo Poesio. 2009. Strudel: A corpus-based semantic model based on properties and types. *Cognitive Science*, pages 1–33.

E. Briscoe, John Carroll, and Rebecca Watson. 2006. The second release of the RASP system. In *Proceedings of the Interactive Demo Session of COLING/ACL-06*, pages 77–80.

George S. Cree, Chris McNorgan, and Ken McRae. 2006. Distinctive features hold a privileged status in the computation of word meaning: Implications for theories of semantic memory. *Journal of Experimental Psychology. Learning, Memory, and Cognition*, 32(4):643–58.

Colin Kelly, Barry Devereux, and Anna Korhonen. 2010. Acquiring human-like feature-based conceptual representations from corpora. In Brian Murphy, Kai min Kevin Chang, and Anna Korhonen, editors, *Proceedings of the NAACL-HLT Workshop on Computational Neurolinguistics*, Los Angeles, USA.

T.K. Landauer, P.W. Foltz, and D. Laham. 1998. An introduction to latent semantic analysis. *Discourse Processes*, 25:259–284.

G. Leech, R. Garside, and M. Bryant. 1994. CLAWS4: the tagging of the British National Corpus. In *Proceedings of the 15th conference on Computational linguistics-Volume 1*, pages 622–628. Association for Computational Linguistics.

Kevin Lund and Curt Burgess. 1996. Producing high-dimensional semantic spaces from lexical co-occurrence. *Behavior Research Methods, Instruments, and Computers*, 28(2):203–208.

Alex Martin and Linda L. Chao. 2001. Semantic memory and the brain: structure and processes. *Current Opinion in Neurobiology*, 11(2):194–201.

Ken McRae, Virginia R. de Sa, and Mark S. Seidenberg. 1997. On the nature and scope of featural representations of word meaning. *Journal of Experimental Psychology: General*, 126(2):99–130.

Ken McRae, George S. Cree, Mark S. Seidenberg, and Chris McNorgan. 2005. Semantic feature production norms for a large set of living and nonliving things. *Behavior Research Methods*, 37:547–559.

Tom M. Mitchell, Svetlana V. Shinkareva, Andrew Carlson, Kai-Min Chang, Vicente L. Malave, Robert A. Mason, and Marcel A. Just. 2008. Predicting human brain activity associated with the meanings of nouns. *Science*, 320(5880):1191–1195.

Helen E. Moss, Lorraine K. Tyler, and Kirsten I. Taylor. 2007. Conceptual structure. In M. Gareth Gaskell, editor, *The Oxford handbook of psycholinguistics*, pages 217–234. Oxford University Press, Oxford, UK.

B. Murphy, M. Baroni, and M. Poesio. 2009. Eeg responds to conceptual stimuli and corpus semantics. In *Proceedings of the Conference on Empirical Methods in Natural Language Processing (EMNLP 2009)*, pages 619–627, East Stroudsburg, PA.

Gregory Murphy. 2002. *The big book of concepts*. The MIT Press, Cambridge, MA.

Mark Steyvers. 2010. Combining feature norms and text data with topic models. *Acta Psychologica*, 133(3):234–243.

Lorraine K. Tyler and Helen E. Moss. 2001. Towards a distributed account of conceptual knowledge. *Trends in Cognitive Sciences*, 5(6):244–252.

L. K. Tyler, H. E. Moss, M. R. Durrant-Peatfield, and J. P. Levy. 2000. Conceptual structure and the structure of concepts: A distributed account of category-specific deficits. *Brain and Language*, 75(2):195–231.

Author Index